ROCKIN THE C# INTERVIEW

A comprehensive question and answer reference guide for the C# programming language including MVC, ASP.Net, ADO.Net, SQL Server and general database, Security related, Entity Framework, WCF, Silverlight and Object Oriented Programming questions and answers.

2017 Edition - Revision 7

By Greg Unger

Ordering Information

Quantity sales. Special discounts are available on quantity purchases by corporations, associations, and others. For details, contact us.

Orders by U.S. trade bookstores and wholesalers, please contact us.

Contact Information

Email address: businessathlete101@gmail.com

Website: http://www.csharpinterviewquestions.com

Dedication

I worked in the Software and IT Industry for over 20 years. I believe in helping others. I believe the best way to do this is to help you as best I can, and give you as much information as possible, so you're not wasting time, making the same mistakes I did.

This book is dedicated to the programmers who didn't get the job because they just weren't prepared. Those who have a hard time remembering reference materials off the top of your head, this book's for you.

Hopefully this levels the playing field and gets you the job of you deserve. If you're smart enough to buy this book, if you're smart enough to know that preparation is always key, then you deserve the job.

"It is by faith that poetry, as well as devotion, soars above this dull earth; that imagination breaks through its clouds, breathes a purer air, and lives in a softer light." – Henry Giles

TABLE OF CONTENTS

Foreword

This book is broken up into sections by subject. You will find redundancy in some of the questions because they cross-pertain to multiple subjects. This makes it easier to skip to one subject or another without any cross dependency. Some of the questions are simple and some difficult. I would suggest you know the answers to all questions even if you just memorize the answer. The answers are short and to the point. If you feel you're lacking understanding of either the question or the answer, I urge you to do further reading. This is your profession and like any profession you need to become a master at what you do. You must know the language inside and out to be the best programmer you can be.

Don't worry if you need to re-read this book a few times. Most people will need to. I find it useful to have Visual Studio open when reading a book like this so I can review in practice things I learn while reading.

I tried to make this as comprehensive as possible without turning this into a reference guide. By no means is this book exhaustive. I could add another couple hundred pages and still not cover everything that could be covered, given the topics I've included. I'm not providing examples and samples to explain the answers. This question and answer reference is meant to get your mind to recall what you already know by giving you short, concise and easy to remember answers.

You'll find I don't group the questions in sections very often. I do this purposely to make your brain work harder in order to commit the information to memory.

CHAPTER 1   INTERVIEW BASICS

Your attitude

Your attitude is going to play possibly the biggest role in whether or not you will get a job. Because of this, you need to be prepared for what your state of mind should be before you sit down in front of the interviewer. As with almost all aspects of life, everyone gets better with practice. To be a top contender for a job, there is nothing better than a successful interview, yet interviews can be intimidating prospects. Here are some suggestions to help you prepare to present yourself at your best.

Assess your skills and experiences

• Focus on three to four areas where your skills are the strongest. Knowing these will help you tell your interviewer why they should hire you.

• Practice describing your special talents and skills.

• Examine your work and education background. Look for skills and experiences that match the job description.

Create a list of experiences to relate

Employers want real examples of how you behave professionally.

• Identify examples that relate to the job description and where you have performed well using your skills and background.

Practice relating the experiences aloud

• Organize your thoughts and communicate clearly.

• Explain the situation.

• Describe your role or task.

• Describe the action you took

• Describe the results of your action.

• Include what you learned or what you might do differently in the future.

• Memorize your answers ahead of time but do NOT come off like the answers were memorized. No one wants to listen to a scripted, pre-recorded message but you also want to make sure you say the right thing.

Organizing your thoughts ahead of time and practicing them aloud will help you to feel more confident and communicate clearly in the interview. Be able to describe your useful skills in layman's terms in case your interviewer is not an expert in the field.

Example:

SITUATION: When I worked at the state library, many of the books were not filed correctly.

TASK: I was in charge of shelving books on three floors.

ACTION: I designed and proposed a new employee training method to my boss. I then presented the new method to the library assistants at the next staff meeting and everyone contributed ideas for the new training on shelving.

RESULT: After that meeting, there were fewer misplaced books, and customers asked fewer questions about finding missing books.

Participate in mock interviews

Practice the interview process to improve your communication and overcome nervousness and anxiety.

I would go so far as to interview for jobs that you don't even want, just to practice. You should be able to work on your demeanor and confidence level if you know going into the interview, it isn't a job that you want. Try new things here and see what kind of response you get. When you don't have to worry about getting the job, you can focus on the fundamentals of being an interviewee.

Mock interviews will help you as well. You can do them with a friend or family member or in a mirror. You do whatever you have to do in order to get the job. This may sound like an odd thing to have to do but you won't think it odd when you get the job because you were prepared. Mock interviews help you get a feel for the interview process. They're also an opportunity to create a personality in your head that you can tap into whenever you're in this type of situation. Being a good interviewee is not about how smart you are, it's about how trained you are and how comfortable you are. Believe me when I tell you that your comfort level will increase exponentially, the more training you have. Practice verbalizing how your background, skills and abilities fit the job you are interviewing for.

Behavior based interviews

Behavioral based interviews and questions have become standard practice. Recruiters ask for detailed descriptions on how you handled yourself in certain tasks and situations. The premise is that past behavior predicts future performance.

Themes for these types of questions include:

• Disagreements and conflicts with coworkers

• Innovative solutions to problems

• Qualities of a team leader and qualities of a team member

• Meeting or failing to meet deadlines

• Responding to criticism from a superior, co-worker, or classmate

• Persuading someone to accept your idea or concept

• Seeing a problem as an opportunity

• Adapting to a wide variety of people, situations, and/or environments

First impressions

First impressions are lasting ones. Often, they are made during the application process, even before the interview starts.

• Voice messages may be the employer's first impression of you.

- The message on your answering machine or voice messaging should be courteous and professional.

- Inform everyone who might answer your telephone that employment calls may come at any time. If you feel your roommates or members of household are unreliable, consider listing cell phone number. Be sure to manage your cell phone calls appropriately.

• Any time you interact with a potential employer or anyone on their staff, imagine that they are evaluating you.

• Be respectful in the way you dress and the way you act.

• Be positive, upbeat and professional when corresponding in person, by mail, phone or email.

• The person answering your questions or taking your application may be the CEO sitting in for the receptionist on a break. You never know!

Dress professionally for the position

• Research industry expectations regarding attire. This could be simply walking through the lobby of the workplace to observe how employees dress.

• Being dressed a little more formally than your Interviewer is acceptable. It shows respect for them, the position, and the company.

• Get plenty of sleep the night before. Your physical appearance will be at its best when you are alert and rested.

• Avoid perfumes and cologne. Your spouse or significant other may think you smell great, but the person who interviews you may not.

Plan ahead to be on time

• Map your route to the interview site.

• Know where to park and how to enter the building. (Do you need a photo id for security?)

• Plan to arrive 10-15 minutes early.

Introduce yourself politely to the receptionist

• Introduce yourself to the receptionist and tell them the purpose of your visit along with your name.

• Thank the receptionist for their assistance.

• The receptionist is one of the first employees of the company you will meet. While receptionists may not be making hiring decisions, they may mention their impressions to the interviewer.

Greet the interviewer cordially

• Greet your interviewer using Mr., Ms. or Mrs.

• Shake their hand.

• Tell the interviewer your name.

• Wait to be offered a seat before sitting.

• Relax yourself to appear friendly and be memorable.

Expect small talk

• Engage in the conversation, be responsive and take initiative.

• Don't worry if the conversation catches you off guard, the interviewer may be testing you to see how you react under pressure. Try to relax and respond naturally.

Many interviewers will begin the interview with casual conversation. This is a prelude to the interview where they examine your responses for qualities the company seeks. One of the greatest things you can do for yourself is to come up with 5 questions to talk about beforehand. On top of that, come up with witty answers and responses that you can make to further the discussion. If this is practiced enough, your first impression will be a great one.

The Interview

Your goal in an interview is to show and tell your best qualities to the interviewer. Understand that the interviewer 's goal is to evaluate you on criteria other than just your skill.

Points to Include in the Interview

• How you fit the job qualifications

• Why you want the job

• Why you want to work for the organization

• What you can contribute to the employer

• What you have learned about yourself and your work

More Tips

• Relate your background and accomplishments to the employer's needs.

• Don't talk about what was wrong with past jobs or past employers.

• Be sincere, positive, and honest with your answers.

• Have your resume and/or portfolio with you in a professional looking folder.

• Avoid mentioning financial concerns or personal problems.

• Take notes during the interview. Make sure you write down everyone you speak to, dates, times and questions asked. This will make you look diligent and engaged and will allow you to reflect upon the interview afterwards. Do not however, ignore the interviewer in order to take notes. Short-hand works wonders here.

How will you be evaluated?

Once the official part of an interview begins, interviewers will carefully listen and evaluate your responses. In addition to your knowledge about the job and interaction styles, they may look for the following qualities:

• How well do you understand the job and meet its qualifications?

• What skills do you use when interacting with others?

• How mentally alert and responsible are you?

• Can you draw proper inferences and conclusions during the course of the interview?

• Do you demonstrate a degree of intellectual depth when communicating, or is your thinking shallow and lacking depth?

• Have you used good judgment and common sense regarding your life planning up to this point?

• What is your capacity for problem solving?

• How well do you respond to stress and pressure?

Refrain from reciting memorized answers

• Present yourself as interested and naturally enthusiastic about the job, not rehearsed and flat.

• Research the position and organization to fit your skills to the job.

• Formulate concise answers.

Maintain proper body language.

• Sit up straight and look alert.

• Avoid fidgeting.

• Smile when appropriate.

• Maintain eye contact when being asked questions.

• Be aware of your tone of voice. Keep it energetic and avoid monotone answers.

Body language says more about an individual than their words. Match your body language to the impression you want to make.

Be prepared to ask questions

• Prepare 3-5 questions ahead of time. Again, being prepared here will behoove you. You will most likely ask the exact same questions in every interview, so be prepared ahead of time. The more inquisitive you are; the more interest you show.

• Ask about the duties of the job early so you can target your answers to the position.

• Pay attention to an employer's body language and watch how they react to your questions.

• Some employers may start the interview by asking whether you have any questions. Others will tell you that they have set aside time at the end for questions. Still, others might be comfortable with you asking questions throughout the interview.

If the interview is not going smoothly, don't panic.

• Some interviewers might test you to see how you handle stress.

• Stay positive.

• Ask your interviewer to repeat anything you don't understand so you can gather your thoughts.

Expect the unexpected

Sometimes questions are asked simply to see how you react.

• Pause briefly.

• Consider the question.

• Give a natural response.

During the interview, you may be asked some unusual questions. Surprise questions could range from, "Where do you see yourself in 5 years" to "If you could live in any time period, which one would it be and why?"

When unexpected questions come up, take note of them either immediately or as soon as possible. If one person asked this question, chances are another might so be prepared with a witty answer next time.

The closing is important

Concluding the interview

• Remain enthusiastic and courteous.

• Ask questions.

• Prepare questions ahead of time to help you decide if the position is suitable for you.

• Leave the interviewer(s) with three things that you would like them to remember about you.

This is also an opportunity to give additional information about your background that you think is pertinent to the position and that was not covered in the interview.

Questions to consider asking at the close of the interview

• What do you want the person in this position to accomplish within the first three months?

• Are there are any important skills needed for the job that have not been covered in the interview?

• What is the time frame for making the hiring decision?

• What are the core working hours?

• Does the position require me to be on call?

• How big is the team I would be working with?

• Is the environment laid back or a bit more rigid?

• What is the dress code?

Questions to avoid

• What is the starting salary?

• What are the vacation related perks, company benefits, or other perks of the job?

Wait for the interviewer to introduce these subjects. The best time to talk about salary is after you have been offered the job. You're then in a much better position to negotiate.

The conclusion of the interview

• This is usually indicated when the interviewer stands up.

• Shake hands and thank him/her for considering you.

• During the interview or shortly after, write down the name(s) of the interviewer(s) so you won't forget.

Follow up

• Thank your interviewer for their time before leaving.

• Send a thank you note via email or hand deliver within two days.

The goal of an interview is to leave a positive impression. Remind the interviewer of your interest, but avoid being annoying.

CHAPTER 2   HOW I GOT STARTED

When I was first starting out as a developer, I remember how excited I was at the mere thought of having any company interested in me. As time went on, and I moved from one company to the next, my salary grew almost exponentially and in a very short period of time. I would love to tell you that this happened because I'm a genius or that I had found the secret to the Jedi mind trick and was able to make people do what I wanted, but that would be "slightly" misleading.

The first developer job I ever had, my salary was $32,000 per year and I was extremely excited! If you do the math, you will find that dividing an annual salary by two gives you an approximate hourly rate of $16 per hour. $16 per hour to do what I love to do was amazing in my mind. Six months went by and even though I loved my job, I happened to see a job posting for another position at a startup company and decided to apply for it. It was a simple HTML developer position. They didn't even require me to be an expert. If I remember correctly, the job description said that I should have "some" knowledge of HTML. Keep in mind it was at a time when HTML was less trivial to know than it is today because standards were still being developed and the language itself was mildly esoteric.

Needless to say, I did the interview and amazingly enough, I got the job. I didn't find out until afterwards that the job paid $64,000 per year! That my friend is a two-fold increase in my salary in the first six months of being a developer! I was ecstatic! You have to believe me when I tell you that this is not an anomaly. You will see later in the book that I am a huge believer in the phrase "Fortis Fortuna Adiuvat".

The new company was amazing. Every benefit you could possibly imagine came with the job. From free gym memberships, to free food and soda, all day long. There seemed to be no end. Who doesn't love and I mean LOVE free food and soda! We had lunch and dinner catered from nice restaurants and even kegs of beer brought in every Friday. This was the life and I was as happy as could be.

Fast-forward six more months. My friend Bill sends me an email with a job description that a local company is hiring for. It's a six-month contract position with the possibility of extension. The pay is $50 per hour on w2 plus benefits. The job description stated that they wanted someone who had at least a few years of experience with Visual Basic and Desktop Applications development. I had neither. However, I had *some* knowledge of Visual Basic and was teaching myself the language from a book called "Learn Visual Basic in 21 Days" that I bought for $15 online.

I decided to interview just for the heck of it. Nothing ventured, nothing gained and fortune favors the bold kind of thing. In the interview, I know they're asking me fairly simple technical questions, none of which I answered correctly and all of which were over my head. I left the interview with my spirit broken and headed directly for 31 flavors to drown my sorrows in ice cream. I'm not really sure what the genetically encoded survival mechanism is that dictates "When I lose the game, it's time to get fat" but I assure you it is a strong one.

The next day, I'm back at my job, just as happy as could be and grateful for even having the job at all, as I sit stuffing myself with Snickers bars and soda. I check my email and see one from the company I just interviewed with that reads:

> *"Greg, thanks for coming in. We have decided that you are a good fit for this position and would like to know when you could start? The sooner the better. - David"*

My first reaction was that the email was a joke on me. No one could have interviewed any worse than I did, nor have any less technical acuity per the job description. It wasn't until much later in life that I understood that most jobs look for a good personality fit over technical expertise and that as long as you seemed confident and competent, you already won 90% of the battle.

Understand that I'm very money driven at this time, so now I start calculating what $50 per hour is, as compared to my current $64,000 per year salary. If we approximate, it turns out $50 per hour is roughly $100,000 per year! My jaw drops and frankly I must have blacked out, because I don't even remember sending the email back stating how pleased I was that they wanted me and that I could start in two weeks. I packed up everything at my desk, sent my letter of resignation and never looked back.

As a side note, that startup company, which had received millions of dollars of venture capital to the tune of about 30 million dollars, having no business plan or any way to make money, went "under" two weeks after I left. I remember talking to my boss a week before I left and telling him that I couldn't believe the company is seemingly doing so well when their only product generates no income whatsoever. I say seemingly because what company would be giving away so many benefits and perks to their employees unless they were doing really well? I wasn't any kind of business expert, but I figured it common sense that at some point one would need a product or service with which to make money. Well, it turns out, management wasn't so bright and less than bright people would give away benefits and perks when they weren't making any money whatsoever. I used to think that people in E-level positions had some hidden genius, but in reality, they're really no smarter than anyone else. This entire experience was definitely a lesson learned to say the least.

So let's look at the timeline here. My first year as a developer I start out making $32,000 per year and am as excited as can be. Six months goes by and I have already doubled my income to $64,000 per year. Six more months goes by and my salary has gone up 56.25% to $100,000 per year.

Think it ends there? Think again. Just four short months go by and I decide that it's time to start my own consulting business and to go find my own clients. I am a diligent researcher at heart. If I don't know something, I am very driven to learn. I will find as much literature as I can on how something is done. I will find any person I can to help me understand the ins and outs of any process. I do as much research as possible on how to start a company and even what kind of company i.e. LLC, S-Corp, C-Corp. After all was said and done, I started an LLC because it was fast, simple and cost virtually nothing to start or maintain.

Tip: Check your states corporation commission website for information on starting your own company, if you're so inclined. It is remarkably fast and painless to start an L.L.C. (Limited Liability Company) You may or may not want to do this if you do any contract work. There are tremendous tax advantages to starting your own business and writing off all of your business expenses.

I attained my first client through word of mouth. My per hour rate? $250 per hour working 40 hour weeks and being my own boss. A 500% increase in salary. I was raking it in, kicking ass and taking names.

Keep in mind, the economy at the time was ripe for this kind of rate and businesses seemed to have no end to their cash reserves. The hype to get their business online drove the need to hire good developers, who could get the job done and companies were willing to pay top dollar in order to get it done.

Luckily, I have always had one true asset about my personality that made all of this possible. The ability to read manuals, no matter how large they were, in one sitting. I absolutely despise reading books for leisure, I always have. There is just something about reading a book for fun that irks me and I could never truly pinpoint what that was, other than to say, I hate wasting my time for something just to get "fun" as my reward. I always need to be learning something new, or honing my skills, increasing my technical acuity and striving to be the better version of myself. Manuals were a way to learn something new, brush up on skills, have more knowledge, and for me, that was the best reward I could receive for my time. 500-page manual on Python? No problem, I'll be done by the end of the day and amazingly enough will retain enough of it to be functional. Sure I didn't memorize the whole thing, but I could learn enough to get the gist and actually start getting work done. By the end of the first week I was coding with the best of them. This is how it's always been for me. If I don't know something, I'll go out and learn it as quickly as possible. I'll try and master it and be the best I can be at it.

Between the age of 25 and 30 my net worth went from negative $22,000, racked up on my credit cards, to a $500,000+ net worth, with thoughts of retiring by the age of 32. I really thought that I just needed 2 million dollars to my name and no debt to retire. I found out later that 2 million dollars might not be enough to retire on. Also, when I say retire, I truly only define it as not having to "worry" about money. I don't think I could ever stop working. It just isn't me.

CHAPTER 3 THE ART OF SALARY NEGOTIATION

This section is incredibly important. It will make the difference between an income of $60,000 per year versus $100,000 per year just by changing your mindset. Your self-confidence, self-worth and perceived confidence will sell the best version of you for the most money every time. Employers hardly ever make their best offer first, and candidates who negotiate their salary almost always earns more than those who don't. I will use rate and salary interchangeably but know that when I talk about rate, I am talking about contract work versus salary which is compensation for full-time employment.

Tip: People who at least attempt to ask for a higher salary are perceived more positively, since they're demonstrating the skills the company wants to hire them for.

Let me stop here and make a quick point. I personally guarantee that if you follow the information in these first few chapters you will get more money for the same job hands down. On a brilliance scale from 1 to 10, I already know you're a 10 because you took the time to buy this book in order to make an additional $1k - $50k just by doing some research. I urge you to help me out, if, I have helped you out. Give me and my book rave reviews to your friends, colleagues and especially on websites like amazon.com and walmart.com. Now back to the fun.

Here's a step-by-step guide to negotiating your best salary yet:

Do your research

Before you go for an interview, you should find out what the market rates are for the job you're looking for. There are salary surveys available online, and if you're dealing with a recruitment agency, your recruiter should be able to advise you on the salary range for the position.

I'm going to repeat the following point a few times in this book to make my point. I strongly urge you to reply to every single recruiter who contacts you for the exact same position to find out what they will offer you as compensation for the position. You may be extremely surprised at the drastic range in compensation you are quoted!

Check online job boards and see what companies are offering for a particular city and area of expertise. I find that general reports on income by profession are grossly inaccurate and misleading. You need to see first-hand what companies are willing to pay. Chances are, the companies that do not post a salary or hourly rate are hiding the fact that they pay way too little. If there is no rate or salary, send them an email and apply whether you're interested or not and ask them what the rate or salary is just so you have a point of reference. The more information you have, the better you'll be able to sell yourself.

Think about what you want from the job, both in terms of the job itself and in terms of remuneration. This will help you appear more self-assured during the interview and salary negotiation process. The more specific your demands are, the better you're perceived and received by the employer.

The newest studies in business psychology show that you're perceived in an entirely different light when you come into an interview with an agenda and knowing exactly what you want out of the job. It demonstrates decisiveness, vision and forethought.

Talk money early

Tip: You should always ask about compensation before any interview. This is usually done in the pre-screen process before the real interview ever takes place. Don't waste your time and the company's time by not doing your due-diligence upfront.

While we all want to earn more when we change jobs, no employer wants to hire someone whose only motivation to change jobs is a higher salary. At the same time, your time is valuable and going into an interview for 4 hours only to find out it pays way less than you would even remotely find acceptable is a waste of your time and the company's time. Make sure you know exactly what the pay or pay range is up front. No matter what a recruiter or a company says, the company has a budget restriction that correlates to a range the hiring manager can work from. You need to know what this range is in order to get the best rate or salary you can.

So, how do you answer the inevitable interview question, "What salary are you looking for?" This is where your homework becomes invaluable. Hopefully, you'll know the market rates for the type of position you're looking for. It's better to give a range rather than a specific number — you don't want to give a salary that's perhaps lower than the employer is looking to pay, but you don't want to price yourself out of the market, either. Emphasize that you're primarily interested in finding the right job for you, and that salary isn't your main consideration. But, at the same time, my immediate response is always:

> *"What is the very best rate (or salary) for this position?"*

Believe me, you may have to ask a few times before you get an answer, but eventually you will get the information you want. The only reason why recruiters don't want to give you this information is because they want to make as much money as possible when placing you. If you don't mind giving away your money, then by all means, don't bother to ask questions. You and I both know, you want as much money as possible for your hard work and time.

Tip: Some recruiters will base what you should receive for the new position off of what you have recently made. This is unfair and frankly is wrong in my opinion. I either tell them that the information is not something I can talk about or I make up a number that matches what I expect from the new position. You are doing yourself a disservice by divulging information that will most likely be used against you.

Some recruiters have WAY more latitude than they let on.

The typical recruiter almost always has the ability to make the final decision on your compensation package. After you negotiate with them, they will need to go back and confirm the package with a hiring manager or supervisor.

In other words, the recruiter is going to sell you to the hiring manager. It's up to them to communicate why you deserve a higher salary. You want their support, because they're going to sell you at a rate that is commensurate with their impression of your personality and skill set. You can help the recruiter out by giving them justification for the compensation you're asking for and by not coming across as greedy or egotistical. The single biggest mistake that most candidates make when it comes to salary negotiation is telling the recruiter what they would be willing to accept. Most candidates don't like being pressured, so they simply blurt out a number they are willing to take — but you should never be the first one to give a number. One way to avoid this common mistake is to ask about the salary range the very first time you talk to a recruiter or hiring manager. If it's not enough, then be nice and give clear reasons for the compensation you do require. You're not battling against them; you're working with them. You would be amazed at what a little time spent negotiating can accomplish. You really have nothing to lose.

I have worked with some honest recruiters in the past and I have worked with some less than reputable ones and take my word, you need to run when you smell a rat. I remember taking a position for a company well under my normal rate just because I needed work fast and the job description made it sound easy with very little responsibility. I went back and forth with the recruiter trying to squeeze as much out of the rate as possible before finally accepting. I ended up with a rate that was $65 per hour and believe me it was a fight to the end to get this much. The recruiter also let me know that I would receive a sign on bonus if I stayed at least 30 days. This seemed sort of odd since I didn't even ask for it but I was more than willing to accept it under the circumstances.

By the third day on the job, my boss let it slip that the company was paying my recruiter $135 per hour! Let's do the math here. The recruiter is paying me $65 per hour and the company using the recruiter is paying the recruiter $135 per hour. The recruiter is making $70 per hour profit for every single hour I work. The recruiter is not only scamming me out of money but also scamming the company out of a much more experienced developer who would readily accept $100+ per hour versus $65 per hour. The company just got lucky that they hired me for that lesser rate. I guess that sign-on bonus wasn't so odd after all.

Needless to say, I re-negotiated the terms with the recruiter and was making over $100 per hour which was still far less than what the company was paying the recruiter! However, I was happier in the end, produced better work and stayed longer because of the additional money. This is a rare thing to have happen to anyone. I got lucky and although I don't recommend doing this, I will say that I would do it every single time, at the risk of losing the job. Sometimes you have to do things on principle, if you have the latitude to get away with it.

It's important to research the company and the position a recruiter is hiring for to try and get some semblance of what the position is actually paying. You will most likely receive emails from multiple recruiters for the exact same position and I urge you to respond to all of them with the following statement:

> *"What is the very best rate (salary) for this position?"*

I think you'll be extremely surprised at the responses you get. The exact same position for the exact same company will have a dramatically different range of compensation depending on who the recruiter is.

Example: I received 10 emails from different recruiters for a senior architect position with a company (Let's call the company XYZ) and to each recruiter, I responded asking what the very best rate for the position was. I was floored by the responses I received which were anywhere from $50 per hour to $125 per hour for the exact same position with the exact same job requisition number!

Shop around and find the best recruiter you can. It makes a dramatic difference. After all, a recruiter represents you and is tied to you for the duration of the contract. If it's a full time position, that's a different story but I leave it up to you to make the right choice as to whether you feel comfortable with the recruiter you're dealing with.

Believe that you CAN negotiate in this economy

Henry Ford said "Whether you think you can, or you think you can't--you're right." Your belief about your self-worth and your level of self-confidence can take you further than any other skill you have. You must believe you deserve the most money you can get from a position. Pretend you're your own talent manager and write down your strengths as if you were going to sell yourself. If you don't believe you deserve every penny of what you're worth, than why should anyone else? You might as well stop reading now, because no amount of information is ever going to help you get ahead if you lack the self-confidence to walk the walk. If you believe it, you can achieve it.

Don't be afraid to ask — But don't demand, either

Know what your worth is and don't be afraid to ask for it. No one loses a job offer because they ask questions — however, you can have a job offer pulled because of the way you ask them. It's important that your salary or rate request is within the ballpark of the range for the position, so avoid giving a specific number until the employer is ready to make you an offer. Remember to be enthusiastic, polite and professional during negotiations. Communicate to your prospective employer through your tone of voice and demeanor, that your goal is a win-win solution. If you're too pushy, the employer may get the impression that you're not that interested in the job (or only interested in the money) and withdraw the offer.

Keep selling yourself

As you go through the interviewing and negotiating process, remind the employer how they'll benefit from your skills and experience. Let's say, for example, that the employer wants to offer $70K, but you're looking for minimum $90K base salary. Explain how they'd benefit by increasing your compensation.

For example:

> *"I realize you have a budget to worry about. However, I believe that with the desktop publishing and graphic design skills I bring to the position, you won't have to hire outside vendors to produce customer newsletters and other publications. That alone should produce far more than $20K in savings a year."*

In other words, justify every additional dollar or benefit you request. Remember to do so by focusing on the employer's needs, not yours.

Make them jealous

If you're interviewing for other jobs, you might want to tell employers about those offers. This should speed up the acceptance process. If they know you have another offer, you'll seem more attractive to them, and it might help you negotiate a higher salary.

Tip: Sometimes when asked, I conjure other offers and interviews out of thin air. I do this to invoke a need of immediacy in order to get everyone moving as quickly as possible and to give myself some additional leverage when requesting compensation for a position. Get good at the bluff, it will serve you well.

Ask for a fair price

Again, you really need to ensure your compensation requests are reasonable and in line with the current marketplace. If the salary offer is below market value, you might want to gently suggest it's in the company's best interest to pay the going rate:

> *"The research that I've done indicates the going rate for a position such as this is $6K higher than this offer. I'd really love to work for you and I believe I can add a lot of value in this job; however, I can't justify doing so for less than market value. I think if you reevaluate the position and consider its importance to your bottom line, you'll find it's worth paying market price to get someone who can really make an impact quickly."*

Negotiate extras and be creative!

If the employer can't offer you the salary you want, think about other valuable options that might not cost them as much. You can look at negotiating holiday days (e.g. if new employees must work for 6 to 12 months before receiving paid holidays, ask that this restriction be waived.), ask for yearly salary reviews or negotiate a sign-on or performance bonus.

Be confident

Remember to use confident body language and speech patterns. When you make a salary request, don't go on and on, stating over and over why it's justified. Make your request and offer a short, simple explanation of why that amount is appropriate.

Tip: It's a smart negotiating strategy to ask for a few benefits or perks you don't want that badly. Then you can "give in" and agree to take the job without those added benefits, if, the employer meets all of your other requests.

Ideally, both parties in a negotiation should come away from the table feeling that they've won. This is especially true when you're dealing with salary negotiations. You want employers to have good feelings about the price paid for your services so that your working relationship begins on a positive note.

Keep track of what you have done well

The greatest tool that you have in any interview is proof. Keep examples of your best work, thank you notes from clients, awards or recognitions, and positive work evaluations. Once you discover what is important to the company and how your skills can meet those needs, you can then use these items as proof of the value you can provide. It's a lot easier to get a higher salary when you have proof of why you deserve it.

Don't take it personally

Easier said than done? Not with practice. Maybe you'll get what you want. Maybe you won't. Life will move on either way. Most people will never have a negotiation that will make or break their life. Keep it real and don't get emotionally involved. If you ask for more than the job is willing to pay, let them call your bluff. It's going to be a numbers game and the more you play the game, the better you'll be at it and the more money you will make for the exact same 40 hours a week. Get the most money for your time!

CHAPTER 4 HOW TO BECOME A REMOTE WORKER

There are three ways to become a telecommuter or remote worker. The first, is if the job requirement states it's a telecommuting position. The second, is to convince your boss that should telecommute and the third, is to be your own boss, so you make the rules and deal only with clients who will allow work to be done remotely.

As a design project manager at a top Internet marketing firm, my dear friend Mary loved her job but couldn't stand the commute. When the price of gas soared to over $4 a gallon, she realized she was spending a small fortune getting to and from her office in downtown Los Angeles.

Mary had been with the company for four years and was already working at home one day a week. Now she chanced negotiating a permanent telecommuting arrangement with her boss.

*"Because our company has a core value
promoting a healthy work-life balance, all of
our major software is available remotely.
Because we have Internet phone lines, I thought
my boss might be amenable to it," she says.
"When I approached my boss, I mentioned my
existing productivity working from home and
how I felt that we could continue to measure
that success while telecommuting full-time. I
promised to be available to my clients during
normal business hours and to return to the
office two days a month for meetings or
whenever there was an emergency."*

Mary spent about 20 minutes coming up with and documenting this letter. That 20 minutes reaped enormous benefits that she would not have enjoyed otherwise, if it weren't for a little self-confidence and the belief that it was possible.

Mary has never been happier. "I get to work from home and also know I have a secure, reliable job." Her arrangement isn't unique. Organizations around the world are implementing telework with enthusiasm. According to a 2014 study by the American Electronics Association, 47 million Americans already telecommute at least one day a week.

BT, a leading provider of communications solutions, hired its first home worker in 1986; today more than

70% of BT's employees benefit from flexible working. The company estimates that it has saved at least $500 million and has improved its productivity by between 15% and 31%.

How do you determine if telecommuting is for you? Michael Randall, a productivity expert, says the best candidates are people who are disciplined and self-motivated: "When your boss says, 'Here's a project, figure it out by this deadline,' do you get it done? Can you stay focused despite distractions and see a task through to completion?" He also says you need to be naturally organized and skilled at time management:

"People who work from home should be able to schedule realistically and prioritize correctly."

If you think you fit the bill, your first step in making telecommuting a reality is to talk with someone in human resources to find out just how your organization's flexible work policy works. Don't despair if there's no official policy in place. There may be others in your department telecommuting successfully, and if you establish a high level of trust with your manager, broaching the issue won't be unreasonable.

To make the argument for telecommuting, prepare a written proposal that puts the organization first and addresses, upfront, the issues you know your boss will be concerned about. The key is to present teleworking as a benefit to the employer.

I was once offered a contracting position in which I explained that I could get the same amount of work done in three-quarters of the time from my own office—without the usual interruptions that come with working in a room full of people. It would also be one fewer desk, phone and computer they had to provide and one more notch in their belt as an earth-friendly employer that does what it can to keep cars off the road.

Your proposal should detail how you'll set up your home office, and it should assure your manager that you will have a clean, quiet and child-free work environment in which to complete your duties. Your boss will want to know that you have a fast Internet connection, a dedicated phone number and all the necessary supplies.

Suggest a trial period for the telecommuting arrangement after which you and your manager can evaluate how it's working. Once you're off and running, make a conscious effort to show your boss that you're cutting expenses and getting more work done faster. Make sure you're always accessible via e-mail and cellphone during the business day, and report often on where projects stand, so your boss can easily keep tabs on you.

Telecommuting shouldn't mean you never see the inside of the office building again. If you supervise other employees, or make presentations about your initiatives, or are a key participant in team meetings, show up in person as often as you can. Telecommuting must not compromise the critical workplace relationships you've spent time and energy building.

If you're currently job hunting and want to get into a telework situation right from the start, you can turn to a variety of websites that list such positions. FlexJobs.com, for example, is a low-cost subscription service that identifies and screens legitimate telecommuting jobs. Just be aware that telework positions tend to be much more competitive, so your resume should detail a history of independent work that produced stellar results.

When searching job boards online, you will want to use keywords like "Remote, virtual or telecommute" in order to find these kind of jobs. Important to note is that I find more often than not, the word "remote" is in many job descriptions that aren't telecommuting jobs at all, but deal with remote (outsourced) teams.

Also keep in mind that most remote positions pay less and are usually salary based, as opposed to hourly, but that doesn't mean you can't inquire about the position and ask if it can be done on a contractual basis. Be sure to send your references and a job history that includes all of the remote work you've done.

CHAPTER 5   TRAITS OF A BAD PROGRAMMER

I don't think anyone starts out thinking "I want to be a bad programmer." Unfortunately, I've uncovered some tautologies of human nature that go against the concept of excellence in almost everything we do as a species. The best example is that laziness is the default mode for most people. Laziness and the knowledge that most programmers can "get away" with doing things poorly at most companies is a strong pre-cursor to forming terrible habits that follow you the rest of your life. I have seen some truly disappointing code and watched the programmers develop software real-time in such a way as to make anyone cringe. I discuss some of these bad habits here.

1) You don't sharpen your axe before heading out into the forest to chop down the trees.

Let's setup an agreed upon context by which an understanding can be reached. I fully understand that sometimes there is no amount of before-hand thought that will afford you the same discovery as just trying to code something in prototype fashion, in order to do some due diligence, or solve a problem. But even a prototype should be an after-thought to at least doing some initial white-boarding when it comes to architecting software at any level. I am not talking about spending a lot of time figuring out how to write a method that will added two numbers. I'm talking about giving some forethought to how you design how the different pieces of your application will work.

2) You don't understand the fallibility of others. You don't understand that you are fallible.

We all make mistakes. If you aren't using version control in this day and age, you shouldn't be hired for any job.

3) People shouldn't have to know your entire history and perspective on life in order to understand your code.

Proper naming conventions and readable code are a must.

4) You love to swim the pool of redundancy.

You write the same code over and over again instead of centralizing it and encapsulating it.

5) You don't think about anyone but yourself when you code.

I see it all the time. Programmers programming code in such a way as to just get things done as quickly as possible. Writing unmaintainable and unreadable code. So much so that the original programmer can't even read their own hieroglyphics. If you have ever worked on code and then walked away to do anything else only to have to come back to your very own code at some point later on in the future and had to take an enormous amount of time to figure out your own code than this is you. If you can't even understand what you did, why would you expect anyone else to know?

6) You don't understand the concept of teaching others to fish, as opposed to giving them a fish when they're hungry.

7) Your ADHD (Attention Deficit) is in full force and controls every aspect of your life.

Scientists have done numerous studies on the human brain and what it is not only capable of but also what it excels at. These studies, over and over, point to the fact that "single-mindedness" allows the brain to do its very best work. Anyone who tells you that they are a hero because they can multi-task is like a drug junky who is telling you that drugs are the best and your life will be so much better with drugs in them.

CHAPTER 6 FUNDAMENTAL C# QUESTIONS AND ANSWERS

1. What is C#?

C# is an object oriented, type safe and managed language that is compiled by the .Net framework to generate Microsoft Intermediate Language (IL).

2. What are the types of comments in C# and give syntax examples?

1. Single line represented by //.
2. Multiple line (/* */)
3. XML Comments (///).

3. What are namespaces and how are they used?

The namespace keyword is used to declare a scope that contains a set of related objects. Use namespaces to organize code elements and to create globally unique types.

4. What is a constructor?

A constructor is a class member executed when an instance of the class is created. The constructor has the same name as the class. It can be overloaded via different method signatures.

5. Will a C# program run on any machine?

No, a C# program will run only on machines that have the Common Language Runtime (CLR) installed.

6. What is machine language?

A computer programming language consisting of binary or hexadecimal instructions that a computer can respond to directly.

7. Can you assign a negative number to an unsigned variable?

No

8. What kind of performance impact does whitespace have on a C# program?

None, most whitespace is removed by the compiler.

9. What is the largest value a variable of type short can hold?

32767

10. What is the result of 9 % 3 in C#?

0

11. Explain conditional operators?

The ?: operator is called the conditional operator. A conditional expression of the form b ? x : y first evaluates the condition b. Then, if b is true, x is evaluated and becomes the result of the operation. Otherwise, y is evaluated and becomes the result of the operation. A conditional expression never evaluates both x and y.

12. What do shift operators do?

The << and >> operators are used to perform bit shifting operations.

13. What are some examples of control statements?

Throw, try, catch and finally.

14. What command is used to jump to the next iteration in a loop?

Continue

15. What is the difference between a parameter and an argument?

A parameter is a definition of what will be sent to a method. A parameter occurs within the definition of a method. An argument is a value that is passed to a method.

16. Can you create methods outside of a class?

No

17. What is the difference between an Array and an ArrayList?

• Arrays are strongly typed.

• ArrayLists are not strongly typed.

• Arrays are fixed length and cannot be resized dynamically during runtime.

• ArrayList can resize dynamically during runtime.

• Elements in an ArrayList can have a combination of combined data types or a single data type. Note: If an ArrayList has combined data types then a type cast is a must.

18. What two purposes does the "using" directive have?

1. Using can be used to alias a namespace to a different name.

2. Using can be used to make it easier to access types that are located in a namespace by shortcutting the need to fully qualify them by name.

19. What is the difference between a using statement and a using directive?

The using **statement** is used to create an object and a scope block, at the end of which, the object is disposed via IDisposable and explicitly destroyed.

The using **directive** is used to reference namespaces.

20. What does the global keyword refer to?

The global contextual keyword, when it comes before the :: operator, refers to the global namespace, which is the default namespace for any C# program and is otherwise unnamed.

21. What are the two classes of exceptions that exist in C#?

System exceptions and application exceptions.

22. Can you inherit from a base class written in a language other than C#?

Yes. One of the features of .NET is that classes can inherit from classes written in other languages.

23. What does data or method hiding refer to?

Data or method hiding occurs when you create a method or data element in a derived class that replaces a base method or data element. This occurs when the *new* keyword is used to create the new method or method signature. It can also be referred to as shadowing.

24. What is upcasting and downcasting?

Downcasting refers to the process of casting an object of a base class type to a derived class type.

Upcasting converts an object of a specialized type to a more general type.

25. Is downcasting safe?

Downcasting is considered unsafe. To downcast, you must explicitly force the conversion.

26. In OOP (Object Oriented Programming), what does composition refer to?

When one class is defined within another class. Regardless of whether the outer type is a class or a struct, nested types default to private, but can be made public, protected internal, protected, internal, or private.

27. What is a nested type?

A type defined within a class or struct is called a nested type.

28. Can a nested type access its containing type?

The nested, or inner type can access the containing, or outer type. To access the containing type, pass it as a constructor to the nested type.

29. Are interfaces reference types or value types?

Interfaces are reference types.

30. What does immutable mean as pertaining to C# strings?

Immutable means the string value cannot be changed once it has been created. Any modification to a string value results in a completely new string instance.

31. What is a reason for having strings be immutable?

Strings will never get a race condition because of corruption. Immutable classes are easier to design, implement and use than mutable classes. They are less prone to error and are more secure. An immutable object can be in exactly one state, the state in which it was created.

32. What is "DLL Hell", and how does the GAC solve it?

"DLL Hell" describes the difficulty in managing versioning of dynamic linked libraries on a system. This includes multiple copies of a DLL, different versions, and so forth. When a DLL (or assembly) is loaded in .NET, it is loaded by name, version and certificate. The assembly contains all of this information via its metadata. The GAC provides the solution, as you can have multiple versions of a dll side-by-side.

33. What is the GAC, and where is it located?

The GAC is the Global Assembly Cache. Shared assemblies reside in the GAC. This allows applications to share assemblies instead of having the assembly distributed with each application. Versioning allows multiple assembly versions to exist in the GAC. Applications can specify version numbers in their respective configuration file. The GAC is typically located in the following directory %windir%\Microsoft.NET\assembly\.

34. How are assemblies managed in the GAC?

The gacutil.exe command line tool is used to manage the GAC.

35. How are methods overloaded?

Methods are overloaded via different signatures. Thus, you can overload a method by having different data types, a different number of parameters, or a different order of parameters.

36. How do you prevent a class from being inherited?

The sealed keyword prohibits a class from being inherited.

37.What is the execution entry point for a C# console application?

The main method. This Main() method is present in every executable C# application. This includes any console application, Windows desktop application or Windows service application.

38.What if we have more than one class in our application with a Main() method?

The class that defines the Main() method is termed an application object. However, it is possible that we have more than one class that contains a Main() method. We can set which classes Main() method will be used as the entry point via the startup object drop down list box, located under the Application tab of the Visual Studio project properties editor. This value is saved in the corresponding .SUO (Solution User Options) file.

39.Why is the Main() method static?

Static members are scoped to the class level (rather than the object level) and can thus be invoked without the need to first create a new class instance. The Main() method is static because it's available to run when your program starts and as it is the entry point of the program, it runs without creating an instance of the class. In other words, static functions exist before a class is instantiated, so static is applied to the main entry point.

40. What is the string[] argument in the Main() method used for?

The string[] argument will contain the command line arguments passed to the application, which are then available within the Main() method.

41. What is the access modifier declaration of the Main() method and why?

The Main() method must be marked private. The reason behind this is so other applications cannot invoke the entry point. The Main() method cannot be declared public.

42. What is the return value of the Main() method?

The return value of the Main() method is void. This indicates no return value and is the default.

43. What is the default access modifier for a nested class in C#?

Private

44. What is the general rule of thumb for access modifier defaults in C#?

The most restrictive is almost always true. The setter on a property does not follow this rule, however. It is public by default.

45. What is the use of the integer return value in the Main() method?

The integer return value of the Main() method indicates whether an error occurred. If the Main() method executes successfully, it will return 0 (this is the default value, even if it defined as void). If the Main() method executes unsuccessfully, then the return value will be -1.

46. How do you set a string literal without escaping each escape sequence with backslashes?

The @ sign in front of the double-quotes escapes the entire string.

47. What does yield do?

When you use the yield keyword in a statement, you indicate that the method, operator, or get accessor in which it appears is an iterator. Using yield to define an iterator removes the need for an explicit extra class.

48. What are some restrictions to using yield?

• A yield return statement can't be located in a try-catch block.

• A yield return statement can be located in the try block of a try-finally statement.

• A yield break statement can be located in a try block or a catch block but not a finally block.

49. Can you have more than one yield return in the same iterator?

Yes

50. What does the "checked" keyword do?

The checked keyword is used to explicitly enable overflow checking for integral-type arithmetic operations and conversions.

51. What does the "unchecked" keyword do?

The unchecked keyword is used to suppress overflow-checking for integral-type arithmetic operations and conversions.

52. What is early binding and how does it work?

The compiler performs a process called binding when an object is assigned to an object variable. An object is early bound when it is assigned to a variable declared to be of a specific object type. Early bound objects allow the compiler to allocate memory and perform other optimizations before an application executes.

53. What are some advantages of early binding?

You should use early-bound objects whenever possible because they allow the compiler to make important optimizations that yield more efficient applications. Early-bound objects are significantly faster than late-bound objects and make your code easier to read and maintain by stating exactly what kind of objects are being used. Another advantage to early binding is that it enables useful features such as automatic code completion and dynamic help because the Visual Studio integrated development environment (IDE) can determine exactly what type of object you are working with as you edit the code. Early binding reduces the number and severity of run-time errors because it allows the compiler to report errors when a program is compiled.

54. What are dynamic objects?

Dynamic objects provide another way, other than the object type, to late bind to an object at run time. A dynamic object exposes members such as properties and methods at run time by using dynamic interfaces that are defined in the System.Dynamic namespace. You can use the classes in the System.Dynamic namespace to create objects that work with data structures that do not match a static type or format.

55. What is reflection?

Reflection provides objects (of type Type) that describe assemblies, modules and types. You can use reflection to dynamically create an instance of a type, bind the type to an existing object, or get the type from an existing object and invoke its methods or access its fields and properties. If you are using attributes in your code, reflection enables you to access them.

56. What is a singleton?

A singleton is a design pattern used when only one instance of an object is created and shared; that is, it only allows one instance of itself to be created. Any attempt to create another instance simply returns a reference to the first one. Singleton classes are created by defining all class constructors as private. In addition, a private static member is created as the same type of the class, along with a public static member that returns an instance of the class.

57.Can a reference type point to an object on the stack?

No, reference types must always point to objects in the heap.

58.What is boxing and unboxing?

Boxing is the process of explicitly converting a value type into a corresponding reference type. This involves creating a new object on the heap and placing the value there. Reversing the process is just as easy with unboxing, which converts the value in an object reference on the heap into a corresponding value type on the stack. The unboxing process begins by verifying that the recipient value type is equivalent to the boxed type. If the operation is permitted, the value is copied to the stack. Note that boxing always creates a new object and copies the unboxed value's data to the object. On the other hand, unboxing simply returns a pointer to the data within a boxed object: no memory copy occurs. However, it is commonly the case that your code will cause the data pointed to by the unboxed reference to be copied anyway.

59.Give an example when unboxing happens natively?

You will encounter unboxing when you use classes designed for use with objects: for example, using an ArrayList to store integers. When you store an integer in the ArrayList, it's boxed. When you retrieve an integer, it must be unboxed.

60.What are lambda expressions and give a simple example?

A lambda expression is an anonymous function that you can use to create delegates or expression tree types. By using lambda expressions, you can write local functions that can be passed as arguments or returned as the value of function calls. Lambda expressions are particularly helpful for writing LINQ query expressions.

*Example: del myDelegate = x => x * x;*

61.What is deferred execution?

Deferred execution means that the evaluation of an expression is delayed until its realized value is actually required. Deferred execution can greatly improve performance when you have to manipulate large data collections, especially in programs that contain a series of chained queries or manipulations. In the best case, deferred execution enables only a single iteration through the source collection.

The LINQ technologies make extensive use of deferred execution in both the members of core System.Linq classes and in the extension methods in the various LINQ namespaces, such as System.Xml.Linq.Extensions.

Deferred execution is supported directly in the C# language by the yield keyword (in the form of the yield-return statement) when used within an iterator block. Such an iterator must return a collection of type IEnumerator or IEnumerator<T> (or a derived type).

62. What is lazy versus eager evaluation?

• In lazy evaluation, a single element of the source collection is processed during each call to the iterator. This is the typical way in which iterators are implemented.

• In eager evaluation, the first call to the iterator will result in the entire collection being processed. A temporary copy of the source collection might also be required. For example, In Linq, the OrderBy method has to sort the entire collection before it returns the first element.

Lazy evaluation usually yields better performance because it distributes overhead processing evenly throughout the evaluation of the collection and minimizes the use of temporary data. Of course, for some operations, there is no other option than to materialize intermediate results.

63. What are anonymous types?

Anonymous types provide a convenient way to encapsulate a set of read-only properties into a single object without having to explicitly define a type first. The type name is generated by the compiler and is not available at the source code level. The type of each property is inferred by the compiler.

```
var v = new { Amount = 108, Message = "Hello" };
```

64. What type is an anonymous type?

Anonymous types are class types that derive directly from object, and that cannot be cast to any type except object.

65. Which members cannot be declared as having an anonymous type?

You cannot declare a field, property, event, or the return type of a method as having an anonymous type.

66. What are extension methods?

Extension methods enable you to "add" methods to existing types without creating a new derived type, recompiling, or otherwise modifying the original type. Extension methods are a special kind of static method, but they are called as if they were instance methods on the extended type. For client code written in C# and Visual Basic, there is no apparent difference between calling an extension method and the methods that are actually defined within a type.

67. Name the two emergent roles involved when using delegates?

Broadcasters and subscribers.

68. What is a thread?

A thread is an independent execution path, able to run simultaneously with the other threads within a given process.

69. What is the difference between Thread.Sleep() and Join()?

Sleep causes the current thread to sleep for the specified amount of time. Join will wait or block the current thread until the referenced thread completes.

70. What are mutexes?

You can use a mutex object to provide exclusive access to a resource. The mutex class uses more system resources than the monitor class, but it can be marshaled across application domain boundaries, used with multiple waits, and it can be used to synchronize threads in different processes.

71. What are abandoned mutexes?

If a thread terminates without releasing a mutex, the mutex is said to be abandoned. This often indicates a serious programming error because the resource the mutex is protecting might be left in an inconsistent state.

72. What types of mutexes can be created in C#?

Mutexes are of two types: local mutexes and named system mutexes. If you create a mutex object using a constructor that accepts a name, it is associated with an operating-system object of that name. Named system mutexes are visible throughout the operating system and can be used to synchronize the activities of processes. You can create multiple mutex objects that represent the same named system mutex, and you can use the OpenExisting() method to open an existing named system mutex.

A local mutex exists only within the scope of your process. It can be used by any thread in your process that has a reference to the local mutex object. Each mutex object is a separate local mutex.

73. What is the significance of the Finalize method in .NET?

The .NET garbage collector handles almost all of the cleanup activity for your objects. However, unmanaged resources (example: Windows API created objects, File objects, Database connection objects, COM objects, etc.) are outside the scope of the .NET framework. We have to explicitly cleanup our utilized resources. For these types of objects, the .NET framework provides the Object.Finalize() method. This method can be overridden and allows an author to clean up unmanaged resources.

74. How do you override the Object.Finalize() method?

You override the Object.Finalize() method in C# by defining a class destructor.

75. What is the use of the IDisposable.Dispose() method?

The Dispose() method belongs to the IDisposable interface. If any object wants to release its unmanaged code, the best way to go about this is to implement IDisposable and override the Dispose() method. Once your class has exposed the Dispose() method, it is the responsibility of the client to call the Dispose() method to do the cleanup.

76. How do I force the IDisposable.Dispose method to be called automatically, as clients can forget to call the Dispose method?

Call the base Dispose() method within the destructor as well as within the Dispose() method. Next, suppress the Finalize() method using GC.SuppressFinalize() method. This is the best way to clean unallocated resources and to avoid the hit of running the garbage collector twice.

77. What is the difference between the Finalize and Dispose methods?

Finalize: Used to free unmanaged resources like files, database connections, COM etc. held by an object before that object is destroyed.

Dispose: It is used to free unmanaged resources like files, database connections, COM etc. at any time.

Finalize: Internally, it is called by Garbage Collector and cannot be called by user code.

Dispose: Explicitly, it is called by user code and the class implementing dispose method must implement IDisposable interface.

Finalize: It belongs to the Object class.

Dispose: It belongs to IDisposable interface.

Finalize: Implement it when you have unmanaged resources in your code, and want to make sure that these resources are freed when garbage collection happens.

Dispose: Implement this when you are writing a custom class that will be used by other users.

Finalize: There are performance costs associated with Finalize method.

Dispose: There are no performance costs associated with the Dispose method.

78. What is the difference between an interface and an abstract class?

• An interface defines what something can do (how it behaves).

• An abstract class defines what something is.

• In an interface class, all methods are abstract without implementation.

• In an abstract class, methods can be defined.

• In an interface, no accessibility modifiers are allowed.

• An abstract class may have accessibility modifiers.

• Abstract classes cannot be instantiated.

• Abstract classes are frequently either partially implemented, or not at all implemented.

• A class may implement an unlimited number of interfaces, but may inherit from only one abstract class.

• A class that is derived from an abstract class may still implement interfaces.

• Abstract classes are useful when creating components because they allow you to specify an invariant level of functionality in some methods, but leave the implementation of other methods until a specific implementation of that class is needed.

• Abstract classes version well if additional functionality is needed in derived classes. It can be added to the base class without breaking code.

• To implement an interface member, the corresponding member of the implementing class must be public, non-static, and have the same name and signature as the interface member.

• When a class or struct implements an interface, the class or struct must provide an implementation for all of the members that the interface defines.

79.What are some properties of interfaces?

• An interface is like an abstract base class. Any class or struct that implements the interface must implement all its members.

• An interface can't be instantiated directly. Its members are implemented by any class or struct that implements the interface.

• Interfaces can contain events, indexers, methods, and properties.

• Interfaces contain no implementation of methods.

• A class or struct can implement multiple interfaces. A class can inherit a base class and also implement one or more interfaces.

• Interfaces can implement other interfaces.

• Interface members cannot be static.

80. What is explicit interface implementation?

If a class implements two interfaces that contain a member with the same signature, then implementing that member on the class will cause both interfaces to use that member as their implementation. If the two interface members do not perform the same function, however, this can lead to an incorrect implementation of one or both of the interfaces. It is possible to implement an interface member explicitly—creating a class member that is only called through the interface, and is specific to that interface. This is accomplished by naming the class member with the name of the interface and a period.

81. Can an abstract class inherit a virtual method from a base class and mark it as abstract?

Yes

82. If a virtual method is marked abstract by a derived class, is it still considered virtual?

Yes

83. What is polymorphism?

Polymorphism is often referred to as the third pillar of object-oriented programming, after encapsulation and inheritance. Polymorphism is a Greek word that means "many-shaped" and it has two distinct aspects:

1) At run time, objects of a derived class may be treated as objects of a base class in places such as method parameters and collections or arrays. When this occurs, the object's declared type is no longer identical to its run-time type.

2) Base classes may define and implement virtual methods, and derived classes can override them, which means they provide their own definition and implementation. At run-time, when client code calls the method, the CLR looks up the run-time type of the object, and invokes that override of the virtual method. Thus in your source code you can call a method on a

base class, and cause a derived class's version of the method to be executed.

84. Can multiple catch blocks be executed?

No, multiple catch blocks can't be executed. Multiple catch blocks can be declared. Once the proper catch code is executed, the control is transferred to the finally block and then the code that follows the finally block gets executed.

85. Will the finally block be called if an exception does not occur?

Yes, the finally block is always called.

86. What is an object?

An object is an instance of a class through which we access the methods of that class. The "new" keyword is used to create an object. A class that creates an object in memory will contain the information about the methods, variables and behavior of that class.

87. What are jagged arrays?

An array that has elements of type array is called a jagged array. The elements can be of different dimensions and sizes. We can also call jagged arrays an array of arrays.

88. What is the difference between ref and out parameters?

An argument passed by ref (by reference) must be initialized before passing to the method, whereas the out parameter, need not be initialized before being passed to a method. The value of the out variable must be assigned to prior to passing control back from the called method.

89. What is serialization and deserialization?

When we want to transport an object through a network we have to convert the object into a stream of bytes. The process of converting an object into a stream of bytes is called serialization. For an object to be serializable, it should inherit the ISerialize interface. De-serialization is the reverse process of creating an object from a stream of bytes.

90. Can "this" be used within a static method?

We can't use "this" in a static method. We can only use static variables/methods in a static method. "this" refers to a specific object instance.

91.What is the difference between declaring a variable constant versus readonly?

You use the const keyword to declare a constant field or local constant. This keyword specifies that the value of the field or local variable is constant, which means that it can't be modified. The static modifier is not allowed in a constant declaration. A constant expression is an expression that can be fully evaluated at compile time. Therefore, the only possible values for constants of reference types are string and null.

The readonly keyword differs from the const keyword. A constant field can only be initialized at the declaration of the field. A readonly field can be initialized either at the declaration or in a constructor. Therefore, readonly fields can have different values depending on the constructor used. A const field is a compile-time constant whereas the readonly field can be used for run-time constants.

92.What are value types and reference types?

Value types are stored on the stack whereas reference types are stored on the heap.

Valid value types are int, enum, byte, decimal, double, float, long and struct. Reference types include string, class, interface and object.

93.What does the sealed keyword do?

When applied to a class, the sealed modifier prevents other classes from inheriting from it. You can also use the sealed modifier on a method or property that overrides a virtual method or property in a base class. This enables you to allow classes to derive from your class and prevent them from overriding specific virtual methods or properties.

94.What is the difference between sealed and abstract?

The sealed modifier prevents a class from being inherited and the abstract modifier requires a class to be inherited.

95.What is method overloading?

Method overloading is creating multiple methods with the same name with unique signatures in the same class. When we compile, the compiler uses overload resolution to determine the specific method to invoke.

96.Can a private virtual method be overridden?

You cannot use the virtual modifier with the static, abstract, private, or override modifiers.

97. Describe the accessibility modifier "protected internal".

Protected Internal variables and methods are accessible from classes that are derived from a parent class located within the same assembly.

98. What are the differences between System.String and System.Text.StringBuilder classes?

The performance of a concatenation operation for a String or StringBuilder object depends on how often a memory allocation occurs. A String concatenation operation always allocates memory, whereas a StringBuilder concatenation operation only allocates memory if the StringBuilder object buffer is too small to accommodate the new data. Consequently, the String class is preferable for a concatenation operation if a fixed number of String objects are concatenated. In that case, the individual concatenation operations might even be combined into a single operation by the compiler. A StringBuilder object is preferable for a concatenation operation if an arbitrary number of strings are concatenated; for example, if a loop concatenates a random number of strings of user input.

99. What is the difference between the System.Array.CopyTo() and System.Array.Clone()?

Using the Clone() method, we create a new array object containing all the elements in the original array. When using the CopyTo() method, all elements of the existing array are copied into another existing array. Both methods perform a shallow copy.

100. How can we sort the elements of the array in descending order?

Use the Sort() method followed by the Reverse() method.

101. What are circular references?

When an object model points to a dependent object with a property or variable that holds a reference to the object that contains it.

102. Why are generics used?

Generics are used to make reusable code classes to decrease the code redundancy and to increase type safety and performance. Using generics, we can create collection classes. Generics promote the usage of parameterized types.

What is an object pool in .NET?

An object pool is a container having objects ready to be used. It tracks the object that is currently in use and total number of objects in the pool. This reduces the overhead of creating and re-creating objects.

103. What are the commonly used types of exceptions in .NET?

- ArgumentException

- ArgumentNullException

- ArgumentOutOfRangeException

- ArithmeticException

- DivideByZeroException

- OverflowException

- IndexOutOfRangeException

- InvalidCastException

- InvalidOperationException

- IOEndOfStreamException

- NullReferenceException

- OutOfMemoryException

- StackOverflowException

104. What are custom exceptions?

User defined exceptions.

105. What are delegates?

A delegate in C# is similar to a function pointer in C or C++. Using a delegate allows the programmer to encapsulate a reference to a method inside a delegate object. The delegate object can then be passed to code which can call the referenced method, without having to know at compile time which method will be invoked.

106. What is the syntax to inherit from a class?

A colon is used as the inheritance operator. Just place a colon and then the class name.

107. What is the base class in .Net from which all the classes are derived from?

System.Object

108. What is the difference between method overriding and method overloading?

In method overriding, we change the method definition in the derived class in order to change the method behavior. Method overloading is creating a method with the same name within the same class having a different method signature.

109. What are the different ways a method can be overloaded?

Methods can be overloaded using different data types for parameters, a different order of parameters or a different number of parameters.

110. Why can't you specify the accessibility modifier for methods inside an Interface?

In an interface, we have virtual methods cannot have a method body. All methods are there to be overridden in a derived class and hence must be marked public.

111. How can we set a class to be inherited, but prevent the method from being overridden?

Declare the class as public and make the method sealed to prevent it from being overridden.

112. What happens if the inherited interfaces of a class have conflicting method names?

The interface method that gets implemented is up to you as the method is inside your own class. There may be problems when the method from different interfaces expect different data, but as far as the compiler is concerned it is up to you. In order to specify which interface method to use, the author must use explicit declarations in the class.

113. What are some differences between a struct and a class?

• Classes are reference types.

• Structs are value types.

• Structs are stored on the stack, causing additional overhead but faster retrieval.

• Structs cannot be inherited.

• All struct types implicitly inherit from the class System.ValueType.

• When a struct is assigned to a new variable, it is copied. The new variable and the original variable therefore contain two separate copies of the same data. Changes made to one copy do not affect the other copy.

• The default value of a struct is the value produced by setting all value type fields to their default value and all reference type fields to null.

• Boxing and unboxing operations are used to convert between a struct type and object.

• The meaning of "this" is different for structs.

• Instance field declarations for a struct are not permitted to include variable initializers.

• A struct is not permitted to declare a parameterless instance constructor.

• A struct is not permitted to declare a destructor.

• Structs are best suited for small data structures that contain primarily data that is not intended to be modified after the struct is created.

114.   How we can create an array with non-default values?

We can create an array with non-default values using the Enumerable.Repeat method.

115.   What is difference between the "is" and "as" operators in C#?

The "is" operator is used to check the compatibility of an object with a given type and returns the result as boolean. The "as" operator is used for casting an object to a type.

116. What are multicast delegates?

A delegate having multiple handlers assigned to it is called a multicast delegate. Each handler is assigned to a method.

117. What are indexers?

Indexers are known as smart arrays. They allow instances of a class to be indexed in the same way as an array.

118. What is difference between the "throw" and "throw ex"?

The "throw" statement preserves the original error stack whereas "throw ex" will have the stack trace starting from the throw point.

119. What are C# attributes and their significance?

Attributes provide a powerful method of associating declarative information with C# code (types, methods, properties, and so forth). Once associated with a program entity, the attribute can be queried at run time and used in any number of ways.

Example usage of attributes includes:

• Associating help documentation with program entities.

•Associating value editors to a specific type in a GUI framework.

120.   Is C# code managed or unmanaged?

C# is managed code because the CLR (Common Language Runtime) can compile C# code to IL (Intermediate language).

121.   What are some characteristics of C#?

• Simple

• Type safe

• Flexible

• Object oriented

• Compatible

• Consistent

- Interoperable

- Modern

122. Can a class inherit from multiple interfaces?

Yes, multiple interfaces may be inherited by a single class.

123. Define scope?

Scope refers to the region of code in which a variable may be accessed.

124. What is the difference between public, static and void?

Public allows the method to be accessible by anyone.

Static declares that the method is globally accessible and can be called without creating an instance of the class. The compiler stores the address of the method as the entry point and uses this information to begin execution before any objects are created.

Void is a type modifier that states that the method does not return any value.

125. What are some examples of modifiers in C#?

1. abstract

2. sealed

3. virtual

4. const

5. event

6. extern

7. override

8. readonly

9. static

10. new

126. What access modifiers are available in C#?

1. public

2. protected

3. private

4. internal

5. internal protected

127. What are the different classifications for arrays in C#?

1. Single-dimensional

2. Multi-dimensional

3. Jagged arrays

128. What is the difference between an object and an instance?

An instance of a user-defined type is called an object. We can instantiate many objects from one class. An object is an instance of a class.

129. What is a class destructor?

A destructor is called for a class object when that object passes out of scope or is explicitly deleted. A destructor, as the name implies, is used to destroy the objects that have been created by a constructor. Like a constructor, the destructor is a member function whose name is the same as the class name but is prefaced by a tilde.

130. What is the use of an enumerated data type?

An enumerated data type is another user defined type which provides a way for attaching names to numbers thereby increasing comprehensibility of the code. The enum keyword automatically enumerates a list of words by assigning them values 0,1,2, and so on.

131. What is encapsulation?

Encapsulation is the packing of data and functions into a single component. The features of encapsulation are supported using classes. Encapsulation is sometimes referred to as the first pillar or principle of object-oriented programming. According to the principle of encapsulation, a class or struct can specify how accessible each of its members is to code outside of the class or struct. Methods and variables that are not intended to be used from outside of the class or assembly can be hidden to limit the potential for coding errors or malicious exploits. Encapsulation, inheritance, and polymorphism are the three pillars of object-oriented programming.

132. What is a field?

A field is a variable that is declared directly in a class or struct. A class or struct may have instance fields or static fields or both. Generally, you should use fields only for variables that have private or protected accessibility.

Data that your class exposes to client code should be provided through methods, properties and indexers. By using these constructs for indirect access to internal fields, you can guard against invalid input values.

133. What is a property?

A property is a member that provides a flexible mechanism to read, write, or compute the value of a private field. Properties can be used as if they are public data members, but they are actually special methods called accessors. This enables data to be accessed easily and still helps promote the safety and flexibility of methods. Properties enable a class to expose a public way of getting and setting values, while hiding implementation or verification code. A get property accessor is used to return the property value, and a set accessor is used to assign a new value.

134. Does C# support multiple class inheritance?

No

135. What does the keyword enum do?

The enum keyword is used to declare an enumeration, a distinct type that consists of a set of named constants called an enumerator list.

136. What is the difference between the private and public access modifiers?

The private keyword is the default access level and most restrictive among all other access levels. It gives the least permission to a type or type member. A private member is accessible only within the body of the class in which it is declared.

The public keyword is most the liberal among all access levels, with no restrictions to access whatsoever. A public member is accessible not only from within, but also from outside the class, and gives free access to any member declared within the body or outside the body.

137. What are authentication and authorization and how do they differ?

Authentication is the process of identifying users. Authentication is identifying/validating the user against a set of credentials (username and password).

Authorization performs after authentication. Authorization is the process of granting access to resources based on their identity.

138. What is a base class?

Base classes are a useful way to group objects that share a common set of functionality. Base classes can provide a default set of functionality, while allowing customization through extension.

139. What are the different types of statements supported in C#?

• Block statements

• Declaration statements

• Expression statements

• Selection statements

• Iteration statements

• Jump statements

• Try catch statements

• Checked and unchecked

• Lock statement

140. What are some different types of caching?

• Output caching stores the responses from an asp.net page.

• Fragment caching caches a portion of page (User Control)

• Data caching: is a programmatic way to cache objects for performance.

141.   What are methods?

A method is a code block that contains a series of statements. A program causes the statements to be executed by calling the method and specifying any required method arguments. In C#, every executed instruction is performed in the context of a method.

142.   What are events?

An event in C# is a way for a class to provide notifications to clients of that class when some interesting thing happens to an object.

143.   What are literals? What type do literals have?

Literals are value constants assigned to variables in a program. C# supports several types of literals:

• Integer literals

• Real literals

- Boolean literals

- Single character literals

- String literals

- Backslash character literals

144. What are the different classifications forerrors?

- Syntax error

- Logic error

- Runtime error

145. What is the difference between the break and continue statements?

The break statement is used to terminate the current enclosing loop or conditional statements in which it appears.

The continue statement is used to alter the sequence of execution. Instead of coming out of the loop, like the break statement did, the continue statement stops the current iteration and simply returns control back to the top of the loop.

146. What is a code group?

A code group is a set of assemblies that share a security context.

147. What are the different types of variables in C#?

• Static variables

• Instance variable

• Value parameters

• Reference parameters

• Array elements

• Output parameters

• Local variables

148. Is C# object oriented?

Yes, C# is an OO language in the tradition of Java and C++.

149. What are the special operators in C#?

• is (relational operator)

• as (relational operator)

- typeof (type operator)

- sizeof (size operator)

- new (object creator)

- .dot (member access operator)

- checked (overflow checking)

- unchecked (prevention of overflow checking)

150.   What is an operator in C#?

An operator is a member that defines the meaning of applying a particular expression operator to instances of a class. Three kinds of operators can be defined: unary operators, binary operators, and conversion operators. All operators must be declared as public and static.

151.   What is a parameterized type?

In a generic type or method definition, a type parameter is a placeholder for a specific type that a client specifies when they instantiate a variable of the generic type.

152.   What is the use of the goto statement?

The goto statement can be used to jump from inside to outside a loop. Jumping from outside to inside a loop is not allowed.

153. What is the difference between a console and a window application?

A console application is designed to run at the command line with no user interface. A Windows application has a user interface.

154. What is the use of a return statement?

The return statement is associated with procedures (methods or functions). On executing the return statement, the system passes control from the called procedure to the caller. This return statement is used for two purposes:

1. To return immediately to the caller of the currently executed code.

2. To return some value to the caller of the currently executed code.

155. Does C# have a throws clause?

No, unlike Java, C# does not require the developer to specify the exceptions that a method can throw.

156. Are the use of exceptions recommended?

Yes, exceptions are the recommended error handling mechanism in the .NET Framework.

157. What does the break statement do in a switch statement?

In switch statements, the break statement is used at the end of a case statement. The break statement is mandatory and avoids the fall through of one case statement to another.

158. Do events have a return type?

No, events do not have a return type.

159. What is an identifier?

Identifiers are nothing but names given to various entities uniquely identified in a program.

160. What is the main difference between a sub-procedure and a function?

Sub-procedures do not return a value, while functions do.

161. What are some ways in which C# differ from C++?

• C# does not support the #include statement. It uses only using statements.

• In C#, a class definition does not use a semicolon at the end.

• C# does not support multiple class inheritance.

• Casting in C# is much safer than in C++.

• In C#, switch can also be used on string values.

• The command line parameter array behaves differently in C# as compared to C++.

162. What is a nested class?

Nested classes are classes defined within other classes. A nested class is any class whose declaration occurs within the body of another class or interface.

163. Can you have parameters for static constructors?

A static constructor does not take access modifiers or have parameters. A static constructor is called automatically to initialize the class before the first instance is created or any static members are referenced. A static constructor cannot be called directly.

164. Is String a value type or a reference type in C#?

String is a reference type.

165. Does C# provide a copy constructor?

No, C# does not provide a copy constructor.

166. Can a class or struct have multiple constructors?

Yes, a class or struct can have multiple constructors. Constructors can be overloaded.

167. Can you create an instance of an interface?

No, you cannot create an instance of an interface.

168. Can an Interface contain fields?

No, an Interface cannot contain fields.

169. What is the main use of delegates in C#?

Delegates are mainly used to define call back methods.

170. What are members in C#?

All methods, fields, constants, properties, and events must be declared within a type; these are called the members of the type. The following list includes all the various kinds of members that may be declared in a class or struct.

- Fields

- Constants

- Properties

- Methods

- Constructors

- Destructors

- Events

- Indexers

- Operators

- Nested Types

171. What is the difference between shadowing and overriding?

• Overriding redefines only the implementation while shadowing redefines the element entirely.

• In overriding, derived classes can refer the parent class element by using the "this" keyword, but in shadowing you must access it by using "base".

• Shadowing is done with the "new" operator in C#.

• Shadowing is assumed if the keyword "override" is not declared.

• A base class element cannot enforce or prohibit shadowing.

172. Can events have access modifiers?

Yes, you can have access modifiers in events. You can have events with the protected keyword, which will be accessible only to inherited classes. You can have private events which will only be accessible to members within its containing class.

173. Why is the virtual keyword used in code?

The virtual keyword is used in code to define methods and properties that can be overridden in derived classes.

174. How can we request that the CLR not call the finalizer for a specified object?

Using the GC.SuppressFinalize() method.

175. In what scenario would we want to call GC.SuppressFinalize()?

A Dispose method should call the GC.SuppressFinalize() method for the object of the class which has a destructor, because it has already done the work to clean up the object. It is not necessary for the garbage collector to call the object's Finalize method.

176. What does the generic modifier "in" do?

For generic type parameters, the "in" keyword specifies that the type parameter is contravariant. You can use the "in" keyword in generic interfaces and delegates. Contravariance enables you to use a less derived type than that specified by the generic parameter. This allows for implicit conversion of classes that implement variant interfaces and implicit conversion of delegate types.

177. What are the approved types for an enum?

The approved types for an enum are byte, sbyte, short, ushort, int, uint, long, or ulong.

178. What information does the sizeof method provide?

It's used to obtain the size in bytes for an unmanaged type.

179. Can pointers be used in C#?

Yes, but they must be enclosed in blocks declared "unsafe".

180. What does the "unsafe" keyword do?

The unsafe keyword denotes an unsafe context, which is required for any operation involving pointers.

181. Why would we use the fixed statement?

The fixed statement prevents the garbage collector from relocating a movable variable. The fixed statement is only permitted in an unsafe context. Fixed can also be used to create fixed size buffers.

The fixed statement sets a pointer to a managed variable and "pins" that variable during the execution of the statement. Without fixed, pointers to movable managed variables would be of little use since garbage collection could relocate the variables unpredictably.

182. What type should be used when handling money and why?

For money, you will want to use the decimal type. Neither System.Single (float) or System.Double (double) are precise enough to represent high-precision floating point numbers without rounding errors.

183. What are jump statements?

In code, branching is performed using jump statements, which cause an immediate transfer of the program control. The following keywords are used in jump statements:

• break

• continue

• goto

• return

• throw

184. What are generics?

Generics let you tailor a method, class, structure, or interface to the precise data type it acts upon. Generics are classes, structures, interfaces, and methods that have placeholders (type parameters) for one or more of the types that they store or use. A generic collection class might use a type parameter as a placeholder for the type of objects that it stores; the type parameters appear as the types of its fields and the parameter types of its methods. A generic method might use its type parameter as the type of its return value or as the type of one of its formal parameters.

185. What are the 2 different types of polymorphism?

1. Compile time polymorphism

2. Runtime polymorphism

186. What's the difference between compile time polymorphism and run time polymorphism?

Compile time polymorphism is also known as method overloading. Method overloading means having two or more methods with the same name but with different signatures.

Runtime polymorphism is also known as method overriding, is having two or more methods with the same name, same signature but with different implementations.

187. *Which namespace enables multithreaded programming?*

The System.Threading namespace.

188. *Can we declare a block as static in C#?*

No, because C# does not support a static block. It does support static methods.

189. *Why would we use the "volatile" keyword?*

The volatile keyword indicates that a field might be modified by multiple threads that are executing at the same time. Fields that are declared volatile are not subject to compiler optimizations that assume access by a single thread. This ensures that the most up-to-date value is present in the field at all times.

The volatile modifier is usually used for a field that is accessed by multiple threads without using the lock statement to serialize access.

190. *Can we declare a method as sealed?*

Only when we override a method in a derived class can a method be declared sealed. By declaring it as sealed, we can avoid further overriding of the method.

191. What modifiers are used when implementing properties?

The get and set access modifiers are used to implement properties.

192. What can we apply the async modifier to?

Use the async modifier to specify that a method, lambda expression, or anonymous method is asynchronous.

193. What is the basic difference between the while loop and the do while loop?

The while loop tests its condition at the beginning, which means that the enclosed set of statements run for zero or more times if the condition evaluates to true. The do while loop iterates a set of statements at least once and then checks the condition at the end.

194. What is the difference between an abstract method and virtual method?

• An abstract method is implicitly also a virtual method, but it cannot have the virtual modifier.

• Abstract method declarations are only permitted in abstract classes.

• An abstract method declaration introduces a new virtual method but does not provide an implementation of that method.

• An abstract method forces overriding to the deriving class unless the deriving class is also an abstract class.

• An abstract method declaration is permitted to override a virtual method.

195. What are external methods?

When a method declaration includes an extern modifier, that method is said to be an external method. External methods are implemented externally, typically using a language other than C#. Because an external method declaration provides no actual implementation, the method-body of an external method simply consists of a semicolon.

The extern modifier is typically used in conjunction with a DllImport attribute, allowing external methods to be implemented by DLLs (Dynamic Link Libraries). The execution environment may support other mechanisms whereby implementations of external methods can be provided.

When an external method includes a DllImport attribute, the method declaration must also include a static modifier.

196. What is the point of marking an object member as static?

A static method, field, property, or event is callable on a class even when no instance of the class has been created. If any instances of the class are created, they cannot be used to access the static member. Only one copy of static fields and events exist, and static methods and properties can only access static fields and static events. Static members are often used to represent data or calculations that do not change in response to object state; for instance, a math library might contain static methods for calculating sine and cosine.

197. What does the "new" modifier do?

When used as a declaration modifier, the new keyword explicitly hides a member that is inherited from a base class. When you hide an inherited member, the derived version of the member replaces the base class version. Although you can hide members without using the new modifier, you get a compiler warning. If you use new to explicitly hide a member, it suppresses this warning.

To hide an inherited member, declare it in the derived class by using the same member name, and modify it with the new keyword.

198. What is an advantage of using get and set to access properties?

It allows the author to assign access modifiers to get and set. You can assign private, protected or internal to the set and public to the get for example.

199. What does CLS stand for?

Common Language Specification.

200. What kind of things can you make generic?

Methods, classes, structures and interfaces can all be made generic.

201. What is an accessible member?

A member that can be accessed by a given type. An accessible member for one type is not necessarily accessible to another type.

202. What kind of things get stored in the memory on the stack or the heap?

There are four main types of things stored on the stack and the heap as our code is executing:

1. Value types

2. Reference types

3. Pointers

4. Instructions

203. Is xml case-sensitive?

Yes, xml is case-sensitive.

204. When a value type is declared within a method, where does it get stored in memory?

Value types get stored on the stack. When they are boxed, a copy of the object is stored on the heap.

205. What is a mutable type?

A mutable type is a type of object whose data members, such as properties, data and fields, can be modified after its creation.

206. What is refactoring?

Code refactoring is the process of restructuring existing computer code – changing the factoring – without changing its external behavior. Refactoring improves nonfunctional attributes of the software. Advantages include improved code readability and reduced complexity to improve source code maintainability. Refactoring creates a more expressive internal architecture or object model to improve extensibility.

207. What are preprocessor directives?

Preprocessor directives, such as #define and #ifdef, are typically used to make source programs easy to change and easy to compile in different execution environments. Directives in the source file tell the preprocessor to perform specific actions.

208. What are nullable types?

Nullable types are instances of the System.Nullable(Of T) struct. A nullable type can represent the correct range of values for its underlying value type, plus an additional null value.

209. Can a nullable type be boxed?

Objects based on nullable types are only boxed if the object is non-null.

210. What is the default value of a reference type variable?

By default, when a reference type variable is created, it is initialized to null, indicating that the reference type variable doesn't currently point to a valid object.

211. What is LINQ?

LINQ stands for Language-Integrated Query. Language-Integrated Query (LINQ) is the name for a set of technologies based on the integration of query capabilities built directly into the C# language. With LINQ, a query is now a first-class language construct, just like classes, methods, events and so on.

CHAPTER 7   C# 5.0 QUESTIONS AND ANSWERS

1. What does the async modifier operator do?

Async allows a programmer to write asynchronous methods. You can avoid performance bottlenecks and enhance the overall responsiveness of your application by using asynchronous programming. Asynchrony is essential for activities that are potentially blocking, such as when your application accesses the web. Access to a web resource sometimes is slow or delayed. If such an activity is blocked within a synchronous process, the entire application must wait. In an asynchronous process, the application can continue with other work that doesn't depend on the web resource until the potentially blocking task finishes.

2. Does an await expression block the current thread?

An await expression in an async method doesn't block the current thread while the awaited task is running. Instead, the expression signs up the rest of the method as a continuation and returns control to the caller of the async method.

3. Does async and await create additional threads?

The async and await keywords don't cause additional threads to be created

4. Does async require multiple threads?

Async methods don't require multithreading because an async method doesn't run on its own thread. The method runs on the current synchronization context and uses time on the thread only when the method is active.

5. Is async the preferable way to write asynchronous methods?

The async-based approach to asynchronous programming is preferable to existing approaches in almost every case. In particular, this approach is better than BackgroundWorker for IO-bound operations because the code is simpler and you don't have to guard against race conditions. In combination with Task.Run, async programming is better than BackgroundWorker for CPU-bound operations because async programming separates the coordination details of running your code from the work that Task.Run transfers to the threadpool.

6. What capabilities are enabled when using async and await modifiers?

• The marked async method can use Await or await to designate suspension points. The await operator tells the compiler that the async method can't continue past that point until the awaited asynchronous process is complete. In the meantime, control returns to the caller of the async method. The suspension of an async method at an await expression doesn't constitute an exit from the method, and finally blocks don't run.

• The marked async method can itself be awaited by methods that call it.

7. Will the absence of await expressions cause compile errors?

An async method typically contains one or more occurrences of an await operator, but the absence of await expressions doesn't cause a compiler error. If an async method doesn't use an await operator to mark a suspension point, the method executes as a synchronous method does, despite the async modifier. The compiler issues a warning for such methods.

8. What type does an async method typically return?

In .NET Framework programming, an async method typically returns a Task or a Task<TResult>. Inside an async method, an await operator is applied to a task that's returned from a call to another async method.

You use Task as the return type if the method has no return statement or has a return statement that doesn't return an operand.

9. Can an async method with a void return type be awaited?

An async method that's a Sub procedure or that has a void return type can't be awaited, and the caller of a void-returning method can't catch any exceptions that the method throws.

10. What does "caller information" describe?

We can get the following information from the caller method:

• CallerFilePathAttribute: Full path of the source file that contains the caller. This is the file path at compile time.

• CallerLineNumberAttribute: Line number in the source file at which the method is called.

• CallerMemberNameAttribute: Method or property name of the caller.

CHAPTER 8 C# 6.0 QUESTIONS AND ANSWERS

1. **What is the null conditional operator as per the following code snippet?**

```
public static string Truncate(string value, int length)
{
  return value?.Substring(0, Math.Min (value.Length,
length));
}
```

It simply checks for a null condition before operations are performed on a variable.

2. **Can the null conditional operator be performed on a value type?**

Yes

3. **Can the null conditional operator be performed on a delegate type?**

Yes

4. *What are auto property Initializers?*

Property initializers allow for assigning the property an initial value as part of the property declaration. The property can be read-only (only a getter) or read/write (both setter and getter). When it's read-only, the underlying backing field is automatically declared with the read-only modifier. This ensures that it's immutable following initialization. Initializers can be any expression.

5. *What are Nameof expressions?*

There are several occasions when you'll need to use "magic strings" within your code. Such "magic strings" are normal C# strings that map to program elements within your code. For example, when throwing an ArgumentNullException, you'd use a string for the name of the corresponding parameter that was invalid. Unfortunately, these magic strings had no compile time validation and any program element changes (such as renaming the parameter) wouldn't automatically update the magic string, resulting in an inconsistency that was never caught by the compiler.

On other occasions, such as when raising OnPropertyChanged events, you can avoid the magic string via tree expression gymnastics that extract the name. It's perhaps a little more irritating given the operation's simplicity, which is just identifying the program element name. In both cases, the solution was less than ideal.

To address this idiosyncrasy, C# 6.0 provides access to a "program element" name, whether it's a class name, method name, parameter name or particular attribute name (perhaps when using reflection).

6. What are primary constructors?

Primary constructors give you a way to reduce ceremony on common object patterns. Auto-property initializers are especially useful in combination with primary constructors.

Primary constructor updates include:

• An optional implementation body for the primary constructor: This allows for things such as primary constructor parameter validation and initialization, which was previously not supported.

• Elimination of field parameters: declaration of fields via the primary constructor parameters.

• Support for expression bodied functions and properties.

With the prevalence of Web services, multiple-tier applications, data services, Web API, JSON and similar technologies, one common form of class is the data transfer object (DTO). The DTO generally doesn't have much implementation behavior, but focuses on data storage simplicity. This focus on simplicity makes primary constructors compelling. Consider, for example, the immutable Pair data structure shown in this example:

```
struct Pair<T>(T first, T second)
{
  public T First { get; } = first;
  public T Second { get; } = second;
  // Equality operator ...
}
```

The constructor definition—Pair (string first, string second)—is merged into the class declaration. This specifies the constructor parameters are first and second (each of type T). Those parameters are also referenced in the property initializers and assigned to their corresponding properties. When you observe the simplicity of this class definition, its support for immutability and the requisite constructor (initializer for all properties/fields), you see how it helps you code correctly. That leads to a significant improvement in a common pattern that previously required unnecessary verbosity.

Primary constructor bodies specify behavior on the primary constructor. This helps you implement an equivalent capability on primary constructors as you can on constructors in general.

7. When are primary constructors bound?

Primary constructor parameters are bound by time. The primary constructor parameters are only "alive" while the primary constructor is executing. This time frame is obvious in the case of the primary constructor body.

8. What are expression bodied functions and properties?

Expression bodied functions are another syntax simplification in C# 6.0. These are functions with no statement body. Instead, you implement them with an expression following the function declaration.

For example, an override of ToString could be added to the Pair<T> class:

```
public override string ToString() => string.Format("{0},
{1}", First, Second);
```

They're intended to provide a simplified syntax for cases where the implementation is simple.

9. What restriction is there on the return type of expression body functions?

The return type of the expression must match the return type identified in the function declaration.

10.Is expression bodied simplification limited to functions?

The expression bodied simplification isn't limited to functions. You can also implement read-only (getter only) properties using expressions—expression bodied properties. For example, you can add a Text member to the FingerPrint class:

```
public string Text => string.Format("{0}: {1} - {2} ({3})",
TimeStamp, Process, Config, User);
```

11.What does "using static" do?

This is a "syntactic sugar" feature. With this feature, it's possible to eliminate an explicit reference to the type when invoking a static method. Furthermore, using static lets you introduce only the extension methods on a specific class, rather than all extension methods within a namespace.

12.What are declaration expressions?

It's not uncommon that in the midst of writing a statement, you find you need to declare a variable specifically for that statement.

Consider two examples:

• In the midst of coding an int.TryParse() statement, you realize you need to have a variable declared for the out argument into which the parse results will be stored.

• While writing a for-statement, you discover the need to cache a collection (such as a LINQ query result) to avoid re-executing the query multiple times. In order to achieve this, you interrupt the thought process of writing the for-statement to declare a variable.

Declaration expressions address these and similar annoyances. This means you don't have to limit variable declarations to statements only, but can use them as well within expressions.

13. What is the scope of a declaration expression?

The scope of a declaration expression is loosely defined as the scope of the statement in which the expression appears.

14. How does the compiler handle declaration expressions with regard to typing?

Wherever possible the compiler will enable the use of implicitly typed variables (var) for the declaration, inferring the data type from the initializer (declaration assignment). However, in the case of out arguments, the signature of the call target can be used to support implicitly typed variables even if there is no initializer. Still, inference isn't always possible and, furthermore, it may not be the best choice from a readability perspective.

CHAPTER 9   ASP.NET SPECIFIC C# QUESTIONS AND ANSWERS

1. How does output caching work in ASP.NET?

Output caching is a powerful technique that increases request/response throughput by caching the content generated from dynamic pages. Output caching is enabled by default, but output from any given response is not cached unless explicit action is taken to make the response cacheable.

2. How is output caching enabled?

To make a response eligible for output caching, it must have a valid expiration/validation policy and public cache visibility. This can be done using either the low-level OutputCache API or the high-level @OutputCache directive. When output caching is enabled, an output cache entry is created on the first GET request to the page. Subsequent GET or HEAD requests are served from the output cache entry until the cached request expires.

3. Does output caching support GET and POST name/value pairs?

The output cache supports variations of cached GET or POST name/value pairs. The output cache respects the expiration and validation policies for pages. If a page is in the output cache and has been marked with an expiration policy that indicates that the page expires 60 minutes from the time it is cached, the page is removed from the output cache after 60 minutes. If another request is received after that time, the page code is executed and the page can be cached again. This type of expiration policy is called absolute expiration - a page is valid until a certain time.

4. What are different methods of session maintenance in ASP.NET?

There are three types:

1. In-process storage (Default location for session state)

2. Session State Service

3. Microsoft SQL Server

5. What is the Session State Service and what is the benefit of using it?

As an alternative to using in-process storage for session state, ASP.NET provides the ASP.NET State Service. The State Service gives you an out-of-process alternative for storing session state that is not tied quite so closely to ASP. NET's own process.

6. What are the advantages to using the Session State Service?

There are two main advantages to using the State Service. First, it is not running in the same process as ASP.NET, so a crash of ASP.NET will not destroy session information. Second, the stateConnectionString that's used to locate the State Service includes the TCP/IP address of the service, which need not be running on the same computer as ASP.NET. This allows you to share state information across a web garden (multiple processors on the same computer) or even across a web farm (multiple servers running the application). With the default in-process storage, you can't share state information between multiple instances of your application.

7. What does the "EnableViewState" property do? Why would I want it on or off?

Enable ViewState turns on the automatic state management feature that enables server controls to repopulate their values on a round trip without requiring you to write any code. This feature is not free however, since the state of a control is passed to and from the server in a hidden form field. You should be aware of when ViewState is helping you and when it is not.

8. What is View State?

View state is how ASP.NET web pages persists data across requests. It handles data that must be preserved between postbacks. You can use it to store page-specific data.

By default, view state is enabled on a page and its controls. This can be a problem as the amount of data and controls on a page increases resulting in more data for ASP.NET to maintain. This is accomplished via the hidden __VIEWSTATE field on a form (look at the page source in a browser), so more data in this field means a slower load time and slower overall processing, as it has to be posted to the server each time. You can limit the size of the data in view state by disabling controls that do not need to be persisted via the EnableViewState property.

9. How can you prevent tampering of view state?

View state can be encrypted to address security concerns.

10. What is the difference between Server.Transfer and Response.Redirect and why would I choose one over the other?

Server.Transfer(): The client is not aware of a page change as no headers are passed back. Transfer to the new page is done on the server side. Data can be persisted across the pages using Context.Item collection, which is one of the best ways to transfer data from one page to another keeping the page state alive.

Response.Redirect(): The web server will send back a redirect command to the client to request the new url.

Context.Items loses its' persistence when navigating to the destination page.

Response.Redirect. While this method does accomplish our goal, it has several important drawbacks. The biggest problem is that this method causes each page to be treated as a separate transaction. Besides making it difficult to maintain your transactional integrity, Response.Redirect introduces some additional headaches. First, it prevents good encapsulation of code. Second, you lose access to all of the properties in the Request object.

11. What are custom controls?

Custom controls are controls generated as compiled code (dlls). They are easier to use and can be added to the Visual Studio toolbox. Developers can drag and drop controls to their web forms. Attributes can be set at design time. We can easily add custom controls to multiple applications. If they're private, we can copy the dll to the bin directory of the web application and add a reference to it.

12. What are user controls?

User controls are very much similar to ASP include files and are easy to create. User controls can't be placed in the toolbox and dragged – dropped from it. They have their own design file and code behind. The file extension for user controls is ascx.

13. What are page directives?

The first line of an ASP.NET page is the page directive; you will find it on all ASP.NET pages. These directives are instructions for the page. It begins with the @Page directive and continues with the various attributes available to this directive.

14. What are some page level attributes?

• AutoEventWireup: Indicates whether page events are autowired.

• CodeBehind: The name of the compiled class associated with the page.

• Debug: Indicates whether the page is compiled in debug mode (includes debug symbols).

• EnableTheming: Indicates whether themes are used on the page.

• EnableViewState: Indicates whether view state is maintained across pages.

• ErrorPage: Specifies a target URL to be used when unhandled exceptions occur.

• Language: Indicates the language used when compiling inline code on the page.

• Trace: Signals whether tracing is enabled on the page.

15. What is a master page?

A master page is a template for one or more web forms. The master page defines how the page will be laid out when presented to the user, with placeholders for content. The MasterPageFile page directive in a content page's header is one way to assign a master page. The content pages rely solely on content and leave layout to the master page. ASP.NET merges the content with the master page layout when the content page is requested by a user.

16. What is the code behind feature of ASP.NET?

The code behind feature divides ASP.NET page files into two files where one defines the user interface (.aspx), while the other contains all of the logic or code (.aspx.cs for C# and .aspx.vb for VB.NET). These two files are glued together with page directives like the following line, which ties the page to the specific code behind class.

```
<%@ Page language="c#" Codebehind="UICode.cs"
Inherits="Library.UICode" %>
```

17. What are .ashx files?

ASP.NET Web handler files have an .ashx file extension. Web handlers work just like .aspx files except you don't have to deal with the browser interface, thus no worrying about presentation. Web handlers are generally used to generate content dynamically like returning XML or an image. Web handlers use the IHttpHandler interface with the ProcessRequest() method invoked when the handler is requested. Web handlers are simpler than pages (fewer events and wiring), so they are ideal for performance-critical applications.

18.What does PostBack refer to?

PostBack is the name given to the process of submitting an ASP.NET page to the server for processing. PostBack uses ViewState to remember controls and data. The IsPostBack property of the ASP.NET page allows you to determine if the loading of the page is the result of a postback event; this is done in the Page_Load event.

19.How can you pass values between ASP.NET pages?

There are numerous ways to accomplish this task; the option you choose depends on the environment. The oldest way to approach it is via the QueryString (i.e., passing values via URL); this is also one of the least secure ways because users can easily see the data and could possibly hack the site/page by changing parameter values. Next, you can use HTTP POST to pass values; these are available via a collection within the ASP.NET page. More specific to ASP.NET is the use of Session state, which makes information available to all pages within the ASP.NET application.

Another approach is using public properties on the source page and accessing these properties on the

target page. Also, you can use the PreviousPage
property of the current page to access control
information on the referring page. The last two require
the source, and target pages to be within the same
ASP.NET application.

20. What are ASP.NET Server controls?

ASP.NET includes a number of built-in server controls
that are the foundation of its Web programming model.
They have various properties to control their behavior
and appearance. These controls provide an event model
where events are handled on the server (whereas HTML
controls are handled in the client). Server controls have
the ability to maintain state (via ViewState) across
requests, and they can automatically detect the type of
browser. With these controls, you will see the RunAt
attribute (RunAt="Server") that signals its processing will
be done on the server.

21. What is the global.asax file?

The global.asax file is an optional piece of an ASP.NET
application. It is located in the root of the application
directory structure. It cannot be directly loaded or
requested by users. It provides a place to define
application- and session-wide events. You can define
your own events, but it does contain default Application

events like when the application starts
(Application_Start) and ends with (Application_End).

22. How can you loop through all controls on an ASP.NET Web form?

You can easily traverse all controls on a form via the web form's Controls collection. The GetType method can be used on each control to determine its type and how to work with it. Now, it gets tricky because the form contains a tree of controls; that is, some controls are contained within others (think of a Table). You would have to recursively loop through the controls to make sure everything is processed.

23. What is a web.config file? Machine.config?

The web.config is the basic configuration file for ASP.NET applications. It utilizes an XML format. It is used to define application settings, connection strings, and much more. These files can appear in multiple directories, and they are applied in a top-down approach; that is, configuration files apply to their container directory as well as all directories below it, but the configuration files in lower directories can override those in parent directories. This provides a way to granularly apply settings.

The machine.config file contains ASP.NET settings for all of the applications on the server -- it is at the top of the configuration file hierarchy, thus web.configs can override it

CHAPTER 10 OBJECT ORIENTED INTERVIEW QUESTIONS

The following are interview questions that are conceptual in nature and deal with object oriented programming in a general way. Some questions will not necessarily apply to C# but are concepts you should know and will most likely be interviewed on.

1. What is OOP?

Object-oriented programming (OOP) is a programming paradigm that represents concepts as "objects" that have data fields (attributes that describe the object) and associated procedures known as methods. Objects, which are usually instances of classes, are used to interact with one another to design applications and computer programs.

2. What are the basic concepts of OOP?

• Abstraction.

• Encapsulation.

• Inheritance.

• Polymorphism.

3. What is a class?

A class is simply a representation of a type of object. It is the blueprint/plan/template that describes the details of an object.

4. What is an object?

An object is as an instance of a class. It has its own state, behavior and identity.

5. What is encapsulation?

Encapsulation is the packing of data and functions into a single component. The features of encapsulation are supported using classes. It allows selective hiding of properties and methods in a class by building an impenetrable wall to protect the code from accidental corruption. Encapsulation, inheritance, and polymorphism are the three pillars of object-oriented programming.

6. What is polymorphism?

In programming languages and type theory, polymorphism (from Greek, "many, much" and "form, shape") is the provision of a single interface to entities of different types. A polymorphic type is a type whose operations can also be applied to values of some other type, or types.

In the very simplest of definitions, polymorphism refers to the ability to create objects that derive from some other object and to allow the derived class to override methods defined on the base class. Think overriding and overloading.

7. What is Inheritance?

Inheritance is a concept where one class shares the structure and behavior defined in another class. If inheritance is applied to one class, it's called single Inheritance, and if it inherits multiple classes, it's called multiple Inheritance.

8. What is a constructor?

A constructor is a method used to initialize the state of an object. It gets invoked at the time of object creation. Rules for a constructor are:

• A constructor name should be same as the class name.

• A constructor must have no return type.

9. What is a destructor?

A destructor is a method which is automatically called when the object is destroyed. A destructors name is also the same as the containing class name but with the tilde symbol before its name.

10. What is an inline function?

An inline function is a technique used by compilers and instructs to insert complete body of the function wherever that function is used in the program source code.

11. What is a virtual function?

A virtual function is a member function of a class. Its functionality can be overridden in a derived class. This function can be implemented by using a keyword called virtual in the method declaration.

12. What is function overloading?

Function overloading allows the specification of more than one function of the same name in the same scope. Overloaded functions enable programmers to supply different semantics for a function, depending on the types, order of parameters or number of arguments.

13. What is operator overloading?

Operator overloading permits user-defined operator implementations to be specified for operations where one or both of the operands are of a user-defined class or struct type.

14. What is an abstract class?

An abstract class is a class which cannot be instantiated. Creation of an object is not possible with an abstract class, but it can be inherited. An abstract class can contain only abstract methods.

15. What is a ternary operator?

A ternary operator is said to be an operator which takes three arguments. A ternary operator is also called a conditional operator. It is typically used as a short-cut for an if...else statement.

16. What are the different categories of inheritance in OOP?

1. Single inheritance: Contains one base class and one derived class.

2. Hierarchical inheritance: Contains one base class and multiple derived classes of the same base class.

3. Multilevel inheritance: Contains a class derived from a derived class.

4. Multiple inheritance: Contains several base classes and a derived class.

17. What are 2 different ways of passing arguments?

1) Call by Value – Passing a value-type variable to a method by value means passing a copy of the variable to the method. Any changes to the parameter that take place inside the method have no effect on the original data stored in the argument variable.

2) Call by Reference – If you want the called method to change the value of the parameter, you must pass it by reference, using the ref or out keyword.

18. What is method overriding?

Method overriding is a feature that allows a subclass to provide implementation for a method that is defined in a base class. This will override the implementation in the base class by providing the same method name, same parameters and same return type.

19. What is exception handling?

The C# language's exception-handling features provide a way to deal with any unexpected or exceptional situations that arise while a program is running. Exception handling uses the try, catch, and finally keywords to attempt actions that may not succeed, to handle failures, and to clean up resources afterwards. Exceptions can be generated by the common language runtime (CLR), by third-party libraries, or by the application code using the throw keyword.

20. What are tokens?

A token is recognized by a compiler and it cannot be broken down into component elements. Keywords, identifiers, constants, string literals and operators are examples of tokens. Even punctuation characters are also considered as tokens – Brackets, Commas, Braces and Parentheses.

21. What is the difference between overloading and overriding?

Member overloading means creating two or more members on the same type that differ only in the number or type of parameters, but have the same name.

The override modifier is required to extend or modify the abstract or virtual implementation of an inherited method, property, indexer, or event.

22. What is the difference between a class and an object?

The term "object" refers to an actual instance of a class. Every object must belong to a class. Objects are created and eventually destroyed – so they only live in the program for a limited time.

23. What does abstraction mean?

Abstraction means working with something we know how to use without knowing how it works internally.

24. What are access modifiers?

Access modifiers (or access specifiers) are keywords in object-oriented languages that set the accessibility of classes, methods, and other members. Access modifiers are a specific part of programming language syntax used to facilitate the encapsulation of components.

25. What are sealed modifiers?

When applied to a class, the sealed modifier prevents other classes from inheriting from it.

26. How can we call the base method without creating an instance?

Use a static method on the base class. Inherit from that class then use the base keyword from within the derived class.

27. What is the difference between new and override?

The new modifier instructs the compiler to see the method with an entirely different method signature effectively bypassing the rules of polymorphism and overrides in C#. When a method of a base class is overridden in a derived class, the version in the derived class is used, even if the calling code didn't "know" that the object was an instance of the derived class.

28. What are the various types of constructors?

• Default constructor – With no parameters.

P a g e | **153**

• Parametric constructor – With Parameters. Create a new instance of a class and allows passing of arguments simultaneously.

• Copy constructor – Which creates a new object as a copy of an existing object.

29. What is early and late binding?

Early binding refers to the assignment of values to variables during design time whereas late binding refers to the assignment of values to variables during run time.

30. What is the "this" keyword in C#?

The "this" keyword refers to an objects current instance of itself.

31. What is the default access modifier in a class?

In C#, the default access modifier of a class is private by default.

32. What is dynamic or run time polymorphism?

Dynamic or run time polymorphism is also known as method overriding in which call to an overridden function is resolved during run time, not at compile time. It means having two or more methods with the same name, same signature but with different implementation.

33. Are parameters required for constructors?

No

34. What does the keyword virtual mean?

It means, we can override the method.

35. Can static methods use non static members?

No

36. What are base class and sub class?

A base class is the most generalized class and is considered a root class.

A sub class is a class that inherits from one or more base classes.

37. What is static?

Binding is nothing but the association of a name with the class. Static binding is a binding in which a name can be associated with the class during compilation time. Also called early binding.

38. How many instances of an abstract class can be created?

None, you can't create an instance of an abstract class.

39. Which OOP concept is used as a re-use mechanism?

Inheritance

40. Which OOP concept exposes only necessary information to the calling functions?

Data Hiding / Abstraction

41. What is a design pattern?

A design pattern is a general reusable solution to a commonly occurring problem within a given context in software design. A design pattern is not a finished design that can be transformed directly into source or machine code. It is a description or template for how to solve a problem that can be used in many different situations. Patterns are formalized best practices that the programmer should implement in the application.

42. What are examples of different "types" of design patterns?

Structural, creational, behavioral, concurrency.

43. What are some examples of structural design patterns?

Adapter, Bridge, Composite, Decorator, Façade, Flyweight, Front Controller, Module, Proxy.

44. Briefly describe the Façade design pattern?

The Facade patterns provides a unified interface to a set of interfaces in a subsystem. Facade defines a higher-level interface that makes the subsystem easier to use. The Facade design pattern is often used when a system is very complex or difficult to understand because the system has a large number of interdependent classes or its source code is unavailable. This pattern hides the complexities of the larger system and provides a simpler interface to the client. It typically involves a single wrapper class which contains a set of members required by the client. These members access the system on behalf of the facade client and hide the implementation details.

45. What does Inversion of Control (IoC) mean?

Inversion of control (IoC) describes a design in which custom-written portions of a computer program receive the flow of control from a generic, reusable library. A software architecture with this design inverts control as compared to traditional procedural programming: in traditional programming, the custom code that expresses the purpose of the program calls into reusable libraries to take care of generic tasks, but with inversion of control, it is the reusable code that calls into the custom, or task-specific code.

46. What does dependency injection (DI) mean?

Dependency injection is a software design pattern that implements inversion of control for software libraries, where the caller delegates to an external framework the control flow of discovering and importing a service or software module. Dependency injection allows a program design to follow the dependency inversion principle where modules are loosely coupled. With dependency injection, the client part of a program which uses a module or service doesn't need to know all its details, and typically the module can be replaced by another one of similar characteristics without altering the client.

47. What is meant by a decoupled architecture?

In general, a decoupled architecture is a framework for complex work that allows components to remain completely autonomous and unaware of each other.

48. What are some commonly used creational design patterns?

- Abstract factory

- Builder

- Factory

- Lazy initialization

- Object pool

- Prototype

- Singleton

49. What are some commonly used structural design patterns?

- Adapter

- Bridge

- Composite

- Decorator

• Facade

50.What is an anti-pattern?

An anti-pattern (or antipattern) is a common response to a recurring problem that is usually ineffective and risks being highly counterproductive. The term, coined in 1995 by Andrew Koenig, was inspired by a book, Design Patterns, in which the authors highlighted a number of design patterns in software development that they considered to be highly reliable and effective.

According to the authors of Design Patterns, there must be at least two key elements present to formally distinguish an actual anti-pattern from a simple bad habit, bad practice, or bad idea:

1) A commonly used process, structure or pattern of action that despite initially appearing to be an appropriate and effective response to a problem, typically has more bad consequences than beneficial results, and

2) A good alternative solution exists that is documented, repeatable and proven to be effective.

51.In testing, what is the difference between fakes, mocks and stubs?

Fake: A class that implements an interface but contains fixed data and no logic. Simply returns "good" or "bad" data depending on the implementation.

Mock: A class that implements an interface and allows the ability to dynamically set the values to return or exceptions to throw from particular methods and provides the ability to check if particular methods have been called or not called.

Stub: Like a mock class, except that it doesn't provide the ability to verify that methods have been called or not called.

Mocks and stubs can be hand generated or generated by a mocking framework. Fake classes are generated by hand. I use mocks primarily to verify interactions between my class and dependent classes. I use stubs once I have verified the interactions and need to test alternate paths through my code. I use fake classes primarily to abstract out data dependencies or when mocks/stubs are too tedious to setup

CHAPTER 11 ADO.NET QUESTIONS AND ANSWERS

1. What are the two fundamental objects in ADO.NET?

The DataReader and DataSet are the two fundamental objects in ADO.NET.

2. What is the difference between a DataSet and a DataReader?

• The DataReader provides forward-only and read-only access to data, while the DataSet object can hold more than one table (in other words, more than one row set) from the same data source as well as the relationships between them.

• A DataSet uses a disconnected architecture while the DataReader uses a connected architecture.

• A DataSet can persist its contents while a DataReader cannot persist contents. A DataReader is a forward only cursor.

3. What are the major difference between classic ADO and ADO.NET?

• In ADO, we use a Recordset and in ADO.NET we use a DataSet.

• In a Recordset, we can only have one table. If we want to accommodate more than one table, we need to do an inner join and fill the Recordset. A DataSet can have multiple tables.

• In ADO.NET, All data is persisted in XML as compared to classic ADO where data is persisted in binary format.

4. What is the use of the Connection object?

A Connection object represents a unique session with a data source. In a client/server database system, it may be equivalent to an actual network connection to the server. Depending on the functionality supported by the provider, some collections, methods, or properties of a Connection object may not be available.

5. What can one do with the Connection object?

With the collections, methods, and properties of a Connection object, you can do the following:

• Configure the connection before opening it with the ConnectionString, ConnectionTimeout, and Mode properties. ConnectionString is the default property of the Connection object.

• Set the CursorLocation property to client to invoke the Microsoft Cursor Service for OLE DB, which supports batch updates.

• Set the default database for the connection with the DefaultDatabase property.

• Set the level of isolation for the transactions opened on the connection with the IsolationLevel property.

• Specify an OLE DB provider with the Provider property.

• Establish, and later break, the physical connection to the data source with the Open and Close methods.

• Execute a command on the connection with the Execute method and configure the execution with the CommandTimeout property.

6. *What is the use of Command object?*

After establishing a connection to a data source, you can execute commands and return results from the data source using a DbCommand object. You can create a command using one of the command constructors for the .NET Framework data provider you are working with. Constructors can take optional arguments, such as an SQL statement to execute at the data source, a

DbConnection object, or a DbTransaction object. You can also configure those objects as properties of the command. You can also create a command for a particular connection using the CreateCommand method of a DbConnection object. The SQL statement being executed by the command can be configured using the CommandText property.

Each .NET Framework data provider included with the .NET Framework has a Command object. The .NET Framework Data Provider for OLE DB includes an OleDbCommand object, the .NET Framework Data Provider for SQL Server includes a SqlCommand object, the .NET Framework Data Provider for ODBC includes an OdbcCommand object, and the .NET Framework Data Provider for Oracle includes an OracleCommand object.

7. *What is the use of a DataAdapter?*

These objects connect one or more Command objects to a DataSet object. They provide logic that would get data from the data store to populate the tables in a DataSet, or to push changes in a DataSet back to a data store.

• An OleDbDataAdapter object is used with an OLE-DB provider

• A SqlDataAdapter object uses Tabular Data Services with MS SQL Server.

8. What is a DataSet object?

The DataSet provides the basis for disconnected storage and manipulation of relational data. We fill it from a data store, work with it while disconnected from that data store, then reconnect and flush changes back to the data store if required.

9. How can we force the connection object to close after a DataReader is closed?

The Command method ExecuteReader() takes a parameter called CommandBehavior where we can specify to close the connection automatically after the data reader is closed.

10. How can we save all of the changes made to the DataSet since it was loaded?

The DataSet has the AcceptChanges() method which commits all the changes since the last time it was executed.

11. What is the basic use of a DataView?

A DataView represents a complete table or can be a subset of rows from a DataTable depending on some filter criteria. It is best used for sorting and finding data within a data table.

12. What is the difference between a DataSet and a DataReader?

The major differences between a DataSet and a DataReader:

- DataSet is a disconnected architecture while DataReader has a live connection while reading data. If we want to cache data and pass it to a different tier, DataSet is the best choice.

- When an application needs to access data from more than one table the DataSet is the best choice.

- If we need to move back while reading records, a DataReader does not support this functionality. It reads forward only.

- One of the biggest drawbacks of a DataSet is speed. As a DataSet carries considerable overhead because of relations, multiple tables, etc., speed is slower than a DataReader. Try to use a DataReader wherever possible, as it is meant especially for performance.

13. What is the difference between optimistic and pessimistic locking?

In pessimistic locking when the user wants to update data, the data provider locks the record from being updated by any other requestor. Other users can only view the data when there is pessimistic locking. In optimistic locking multiple users can open the same record for updating, thus increasing maximum concurrency. A record is only locked when updating the record. This is the most preferred way of locking practically. Nowadays, in browser based applications this is very common, and pessimistic locking is not a practical solution.

14. What is the difference between the Dataset.Clone() method and Dataset.Copy()?

Clone: It only copies the structure; it does not copy data.

Copy: Copies both the structure and data (Deep copy)

15. What is the maximum pool size in an ADO.NET Connection String used for?

The maximum pool size decides the maximum number of connection objects to be pooled. If the maximum pool size is reached and there is no usable connection available, the request is queued until connections are released back into the pool. So it's always a good habit to call the Close or Dispose method of the connection as soon as you have finished working with the Connection object.

16. What is connection pooling?

Connection pooling reduces the number of times that new connections must be opened. The pooler maintains ownership of the physical connection. It manages connections by keeping alive a set of active connections for each given connection configuration. Whenever a user calls Open() on a connection, the pooler looks for an available connection in the pool. If a pooled connection is available, it returns it to the caller instead of opening a new connection. When the application calls Close() on the connection, the pooler returns it to the pooled set of active connections instead of closing it. Once the connection is returned to the pool, it is ready to be reused on the next Open() call.

CHAPTER 12 SQL AND DATABASE QUESTIONS AND ANSWERS

Let's start out with some Business Intelligence (BI) terms that you should know. Just knowing what the acronym means is sometimes enough for an interviewer. I highly suggest you know what these terms are and do some additional research into any of these that show up on your job requirement.

OLAP: Online analytical processing

MDA: Multi-Dimensional Analytics

MDX: Multi-Dimensional Expressions

OLTP: Online Transaction Processing

SSIS: SQL Server Integration Services

SSRS: SQL Server Reporting Services

CTE: WITH statements: Common Table Expressions

BIDS: Business Intelligence Development Studio

DML: Data Manipulation language – covers CRUD operations

CRUD: Create Read Update Delete

DDL: Data Definition Language – Language used to create database objects such as tables, view, etc.

SAAS: Software as a service just like APS (Application Service Provider)

Materialized View: An indexed view because once indexed it is persisted to disk.

ETL: Extraction, Transformation and Loading: an acronym used to describe a set of tools for moving data between various database systems. In order to move the data, it must be extracted, often transformed and then loaded into a target. Data Junction, Carleton, Intellidex are some early players in this space.

EDI: Electronic Data Interchange is a specification for exchanging electronic data documents based on EDIFECS. This is basically a way of exchanging orders, receipts and confirmations of orders, used in everything from retail to government procurement installations. It is a fairly old specification and has a pretty large base of users (who are constantly attempting to migrate off the standard)

1. *What does OLAP consists of?*

Consolidation (Roll-up), Drill down, slicing and dicing.

2. *Explain Consolidation in the context of BI?*

Consolidation involves the aggregation of data that can be accumulated and computed in one or more dimensions.

3. *What is a FACT table in data warehousing?*

A fact table is the central table in a "star schema" of a data warehouse. A fact table stores quantitative information for analysis and is often denormalized.

A fact table is mainly made up of Foreign key column which references to various dimension and numeric measure values on which aggregation will be performed. Fact tables are of different types, E.g. Transactional, Cumulative and Snapshot.

4. *What are measure and measure groups in BI?*

A metrics value stored in your Fact Table is called a measure. Measures are used to analyze performance of the business. A measure usually contains numeric data, which can be aggregated against the usage of an associated dimensions. A measure group holds a collection of related measures.

5. What are tuples in BI?

A tuple uniquely identifies a slice of data from a cube. The tuple is formed by a combination of dimension members, as long as there are no two or more members that belong to the same hierarchy.

6. What are the types of SQL Server constraints?

1. Unique Constraint: Column may not contain duplicate values

2. CHECK Constraint: Allow you to specify a value that the database will use to populate fields that are created and left blank

3. NOT NULL constraint: Allow you to specify that a column may not contain NULL values.

4. PRIMARY KEY constraint: specify fields that uniquely identify each record in the table.

5. FOREIGN KEY constraint: are fields in a relational database table that match the primary key column of another table. Foreign keys can be used to cross-reference tables.

7. *What is the difference between a Primary Key and a Unique Key constraint?*

- Primary key:

  - Doesn't allow null values.

  - By default it adds a clustered index

  - A table can have only 1 primary key

  - Are the target of foreign key constraints.

- Unique key:

  - Allows null value, but only one key can be null.

  - By default it adds a unique non-clustered index.

  - You can define multiple unique keys.

8. *What are the types of indexes in SQL Server?*

1. Hash

With a hash index, data is accessed through an in-memory hash table. Hash indexes consume a fixed amount of memory, which is a function of the bucket count.

2. Memory-optimized non-clustered indexes

For memory-optimized non-clustered indexes, memory consumption is a function of the row count and the size of the index key columns.

3. Clustered

A clustered index sorts and stores the data rows of the table or view in order based on the clustered index key. The clustered index is implemented as a B-tree index structure that supports fast retrieval of the rows, based on their clustered index key values.

4. Non-clustered

A non-clustered index can be defined on a table or view with a clustered index or on a heap. Each index row in the non-clustered index contains the non-clustered key value and a row locator. This locator points to the data row in the clustered index or heap having the key value. The rows in the index are stored in the order of the index key values, but the data rows are not guaranteed to be in any particular order unless a clustered index is created on the table.

5. Unique

A unique index ensures that the index key contains no duplicate values and therefore every row in the table or view is in some way unique.

Uniqueness can be a property of both clustered and non-clustered indexes.

6. Columnstore

An in-memory columnstore index stores and manages data by using column-based data storage and column-based query processing.

Columnstore indexes work well for data warehousing workloads that primarily perform bulk loads and read-only queries. Use the columnstore index to achieve up to 10x query performance gains over traditional row-oriented storage, and up to 7x data compression over the uncompressed data size.

7. Index with included columns

A non-clustered index that is extended to include nonkey columns in addition to the key columns.

8. Index on computed columns

An index on a column that is derived from the value of one or more other columns, or certain deterministic inputs.

9. Filtered

An optimized non-clustered index, especially suited to cover queries that select from a well-defined subset of data. It uses a filter predicate to index a portion of rows in the table. A well-designed filtered index can improve query performance, reduce index maintenance costs, and reduce index storage costs compared with full-table indexes.

10. Spatial

A spatial index provides the ability to perform certain operations more efficiently on spatial objects (spatial data) in a column of the geometry data type. The spatial index reduces the number of objects on which relatively costly spatial operations need to be applied.

11. XML

A shredded, and persisted, representation of the XML binary large objects (BLOBs) in the xml data type column.

12. Full-text

A special type of token-based functional index that is built and maintained by the Microsoft Full-Text Engine for SQL Server. It provides efficient support for sophisticated word searches in character string.

9. What are the types of JOINS in SQL Server?

1. Inner Join

Inner join returns only those records/rows that match/exists in both the tables.

2. Left Outer Join

A left outer join returns all records/rows from the left table and from the right table returns only matched records. If there are no columns matching in the right table, it returns NULL values.

3. Right Outer Join

A right outer join returns all records/rows from the right table and from the left table returns only matched records. If there are no columns matching in the left table, it returns NULL values.

4. Full Outer Join

A full outer join combines a left outer join and a right outer join. This join returns all records/rows from both the tables. If there are no columns matching in either table, it returns NULL values.

5. Self Join

A self join is used to join a database table to itself, particularly when the table has a Foreign key that references its own Primary Key. Basically we have only three types of joins: Inner join, Outer join and Cross join. We use any of these three JOINS to join a table to itself. Hence, self join is not a "type" of sql join.

6. Cross Join

A cross join is a Cartesian join which means a Cartesian product of both the tables. This join does not need any condition to join two tables. This join returns records/rows that are a multiplication of records from both tables.

10. What does denormalization mean?

Denormalization is the process of attempting to optimize the read performance of a database by adding redundant data or by grouping data. In some cases, denormalization is a means of addressing performance or scalability in relational database software.

Databases intended for online transaction processing (OLTP) are typically more **normalized** than databases intended for online analytical processing (OLAP). OLTP applications are characterized by a high volume of small transactions such as updating a sales record at a supermarket checkout counter. The expectation is that each transaction will leave the database in a consistent state. By contrast, databases intended for OLAP operations are primarily "read mostly" databases. OLAP applications tend to extract historical data that has accumulated over a long period of time. For such databases, redundant or "denormalized" data may facilitate business intelligence applications.

11. What does database normalization refer to?

Database normalization is the process of organizing the fields and tables of a relational database to minimize redundancy. Normalization usually involves dividing large tables into smaller (and less redundant) tables and defining relationships between them. The objective is to isolate data so that additions, deletions, and modifications of a field can be made in just one table and then propagated through the rest of the database using the defined relationships.

12. What is Microsoft DTS?

Microsoft SQL Server Data Transformation Services (DTS) is a set of graphical tools and programmable objects that lets you extract, transform, and consolidate data from disparate sources into single or multiple destinations.

13. What does fill factor refer to?

Fill factor is the value that determines the percentage of space on each leaf-level page to be filled with data. In SQL Server, the smallest unit is a page. Every page can store one or more rows based on the size of the row. The default value of the Fill factor is 100, which is same as a value of 0. The default Fill Factor (100 or 0) will allow the SQL Server to fill the leaf-level pages of an index with the maximum numbers of the rows it can fit. There will be no or very little empty space left in the page when the fill factor is 100.

14. What is the difference between DELETE, TRUNCATE and DROP in SQL Server?

The DELETE command is used to remove rows from a table. A WHERE clause can be used to only remove some rows. If no WHERE condition is specified, all rows will be removed. After performing a DELETE operation, you need to COMMIT or ROLLBACK the transaction to make the change permanent or to undo it. Note that this operation will cause all DELETE triggers on the table to fire.

TRUNCATE removes all rows from a table. The operation cannot be rolled back and no triggers will be fired. As such, TRUCATE is faster and doesn't use as much undo space as a DELETE.

The DROP command removes a table from the database. All the table rows, indexes and privileges will also be removed. No DML triggers will be fired. The operation cannot be rolled back.

15. Why can't a table have two clustered indexes?

The short answer? A clustered index is the table. When you define a clustered index on a table, the database engine sorts all the rows in the table, in ascending or descending order, based on the columns identified in the index definition (the key columns). The clustered index is not a separate entity like it is with other index types, but rather a mechanism for sorting the table and facilitating quick data access.

16. Given the many benefits of clustered tables, why even bother with heaps?

Clustered tables are great, and most of your queries will probably perform best of your tables are configured with clustered indexes. But in some cases you might want to leave the table in its natural state, as a heap, and create only non-clustered index to support your queries.

A heap, as you'll recall, stores data in an unspecified order. Normally, the database engine adds the data in the order the rows are inserted into the table, although the engine likes to move rows around on occasion to store them more efficiently. As a result, you have no way to predict how the data will be ordered.

If the query engine must find data without the benefit of a non-clustered index, it does a full table scan to locate the target rows. On a very small table, this is usually not a big deal, but as a heap grows in size, performance is likely to quickly degrade. A non-clustered index can help by using a pointer that directs the query engine to the file, page, and row where the data is stored—normally a far better alternative to a table scan. Even so, it's still hard to beat the benefits of a clustered index when weighing query performance.

Yet heaps can help improve performance in certain situations. Consider the table that has a lot of insert activity, but few updates and deletes, if any. For example, a table that stores log data is likely restricted mostly to insert operations, until perhaps the data is archived. On a heap, you won't see the type of page splits and fragmentation you would with a clustered index (depending on the key columns) because rows are simply added to the end of the heap. Too much page splitting can have a significant effect on performance, and not in a good way. In general, heaps make insert operations relatively painless, and you don't have to contend with the storage or maintenance overhead you find with clustered indexes.

But the lack of updates and deletions should not be the only considerations. The way in which data is retrieved is also an important factor. For example, you should not use a heap if you frequently query ranges of data or the queried data must often be sorted or grouped.

What all this means is that you should consider using a heap only when you're working with ultra-light tables or your DML operations are limited to inserts and your queries are fairly basic (and you're still using non-clustered indexes). Otherwise, stick with a well-designed clustered index. One defined on a simple ascending key, such as the ubiquitous IDENTITY column.

17. Can you create a clustered index on a column with duplicate values?

Yes and no. Yes, you can create a clustered index on key columns that contain duplicate values. No, the key columns cannot remain in a non-unique state. Let me explain. If you create a non-unique clustered index on a column, the database engine adds a four-byte integer (uniquifier) to duplicate values to ensure their uniqueness and, subsequently, to provide a way to identify each row in the clustered table.

For example, you might decide to create a clustered index on the LastName column of a table that contains customer data. The column includes the values Franklin, Hancock, Washington, and Smith. You then insert the values Adams, Hancock, Smith, and Smith. Because the values in the key column must ultimately be unique, the database engine will modify the duplicates so that the values look something like this: Adams, Franklin, Hancock, Hancock1234, Washington, Smith, Smith4567, and Smith5678.

On the surface, this might seem an okay approach, but the integer increases the size of the key values, which could start becoming an issue if you have a lot of duplicate values and those values are being referenced by foreign keys and non-clustered indexes. For this reason, you should try to create unique clustered indexes whenever possible. If not possible, at least go for columns that have a high percentage of unique values.

18. How is a table stored if a clustered index has not been defined on the table?

SQL Server essentially supports two types of tables: a clustered table, one on which a clustered index has been defined, and a heap table, or just plain heap. Unlike a clustered table, data within a heap is not ordered in any way. It is essentially a pile of data. If you add a row to the table, the database engine simply tacks it at the end of the page. When the page fills, data is added to a new page.

In most cases, you'll want to create a clustered index on a table to take advantage of the sorting capabilities and query benefits they can deliver. (Consider what it would be like to find a number in a phone book if it were not sorted in any way.) However, if you choose not to create a clustered index, you can still create non--clustered indexes on the heap. In such cases, each row in the index includes a pointer that identifies the row being referenced in the heap. The pointer includes the data file ID, page number, and row number for the targeted data.

19. What is the relationship between unique and primary key constraints and a table's indexes?

Primary key and unique constraints ensure that the values in the key columns are unique. You can define only one primary key on a table and it cannot contain null values. You can create multiple unique constraints on a table and each one can contain a single null value.

When you create a primary key constraint, the database engine also creates a unique clustered index, if a clustered index doesn't already exist. However, you can override the default behavior and specify that a non-clustered index be created. If a clustered index does exist when you create the primary key, the database engine creates a unique non-clustered index.

When you create a unique constraint, the database engine creates a unique non-clustered index. However, you can specify that a unique clustered index be created if a clustered index does not already exist. For all practical purposes, a unique constraint and unique index are one in the same.

20. In SQL Server, why are clustered and non-clustered indexes considered B-tree indexes?

A basic SQL Server index, whether clustered or non-clustered, is spread across a set of pages, referred to as the index nodes. These pages are organized into a hierarchical B-tree structure. At the top sits the root node, at the bottom, the leaf nodes, with intermediate nodes in between.

The root node represents the main entry point for queries trying to locate data via the index. From that node, the query engine negotiates the hierarchy down to the appropriate leaf node, where the actual data resides.

For example, suppose your query is looking for the row that contains the key value 82. The query engine starts at the root node, which points to the correct intermediate node, in this case, the 1-100 node. From the 1-100 node, the engine proceeds to the 51-100 node, and from there, goes to the 76-100 leaf node. If this is a clustered index, the leaf node will contain the entire row of data associated with the key value 82. If this is a non-clustered index, the leaf node will point to the clustered table or heap where the row exists.

21.How can an index improve performance if the query engine has to negotiate through all those index nodes?

First off, indexes do not always improve performance. Too many of the wrong type of indexes can bog down a system and make query performance worse. That said, if indexes have been carefully implemented, they can provide a significant performance boost.

Think of a big fat book about SQL Server performance tuning. Imagine that you want to find information about configuring the Resource Governor. You can thumb through the book one page at a time, or you can go to the index and find the exact page number where the information is located (assuming the book has been properly indexed). Undoubtedly, this could save you a considerable amount of time, despite the fact that you must refer to an entirely different structure (the index) to get the information you need from the primary structure (the book).

Just like a book's index, a SQL Server index lets you perform targeted queries instead of scanning all of a table's data. For small tables, a full scan is usually not a big deal, but large tables spread across many data pages can result in excessively long-running queries if no index exists to point the query engine in the right direction. Imagine being lost on the Los Angeles freeways at rush hour without a map, and you will get the idea.

22. If indexes are so great, why not just create them on every column?

No good deed goes unpunished. At least that's how it works with indexes. Sure, they're great as long as all you run are SELECT statements against the database, but throw in a lot of INSERT, UPDATE, and DELETE statements, and the landscape quickly changes.

When you issue a SELECT statement, the query engine finds the index, navigates the B-tree structure, and locates the desired data. What could be simpler? But that all changes if you issue a data modification statement, such as UPDATE. True, for the first part of the UPDATE operation, the query engine can again use the index to locate the row to be modified. That's the good news. And if it's a simple update and no key values are involved, chances are the process will be fairly painless. But if the update forces a page split or key values change and get moved to different nodes, the index might need to be reorganized, impacting other indexes and operations and resulting in slower performance all around.

Same with a DELETE statement. An index can help locate the data to be deleted, but the deletion itself might result in page reshuffling. And as for the INSERT statement, it's the sworn enemy of all indexes. You start adding a lot of data and your indexes have to be modified and reorganized and everybody suffers.

So the way in which your database is queried must be uppermost in your thinking when determining what sort of indexes to add and how many. More is not necessarily better. Before you throw another index at a table, consider the costs, not only on query performance, but also on disk space, index maintenance, and the domino effects on other operations. Your index strategy is one of the most important aspects of a successful database implementation and should take into account a number of considerations, from index size to the number of unique values to the type of queries being supported.

23. Does a clustered index have to be created on the primary key column?

You can create a clustered index on any qualified columns. True, a clustered index and primary key constraint is usually a match made in heaven, so well suited in fact that when you define a primary key, a clustered index is automatically created, if one doesn't already exist. Still, you might decide that the clustered index would be better matched elsewhere, and often your decision would be justified.

The main purpose of a clustered index is to sort all the rows in your table, based on the key columns in your index definition, and provide quick and easy access to the table's data. The table's primary key can be a good choice because it uniquely identifies every row in the table, without the need for additional data. In some cases, a surrogate primary key can be an even better choice because, in addition to being unique, the values are small and added sequentially, making the non-clustered indexes that reference those values more efficient as well. The query optimizer also loves such an arrangement because joins can be processed faster, as can queries that in some other way reference the primary key and its associated clustered index. As I said, a match made in heaven.

In the end, however, your clustered index should take into account a number of factors, such as how many non-clustered indexes will be pointing to the clustered index, how often the clustered key values will change and how large those key columns are. When the values in a clustered index change or the index doesn't perform well, all of the other tables' indexes can be impacted. A clustered index should be based on relatively stable columns that grow in an orderly fashion, as opposed to growing randomly. The index should also support the queries most commonly accessing the table's data so they can take full advantage of the data being sorted and available in the leaf nodes. If the primary key fits this scenario, then use it. Otherwise, use a different set of columns.

24. If you index a view is it still a view?

A view is a virtual table made up a data from one or more other tables. It is essentially a named query that retrieves the data from the underlying tables when you call that view. You can improve a view's performance by creating clustered and non-clustered indexes on that view, just like you create indexes on a table, the main caveat being that you must create a unique clustered index before you can create a non-clustered one.

When creating an indexed view (also referred to as a materialized view), the view definition itself remains a separate entity. It is, after all, merely a hard-coded SELECT statement stored in the database. The indexes are a different story. Whether you create a clustered or non-clustered index, the data is persisted to disk, just like a regular index. In addition, when the data in the underlying tables change, the indexes are automatically updated (which means you might want to avoid indexing views where the underlying data changes frequently). In any case, the view itself still remains a view, but one that just happens to have indexes associated with it.

Before you can create an index on a view, it must meet a number of restrictions. For example, the view can reference only base tables, not other views, and those tables must be within the same database. There are lots more restrictions, of course, so be sure to refer to the SQL Server documentation for all the sordid details.

25. Why would you use a covering index instead of a composite index?

First, let's make sure we understand the differences between them. A composite index is simply one in which you include more than one key column. Multiple key columns can be useful for uniquely identifying a row, as can be the case when a unique cluster is defined on a primary key, or you're trying to optimize an often-used query that references multiple columns. In general, however, the more key columns an index contains, the less efficient that index, which means composite indexes should be used judiciously.

That said, there are times when a query would benefit greatly if all the referenced columns were located on the same leaf nodes as the index. This is not an issue for clustered indexes because all data is already three. (That's why it's so important to give plenty of thought to how you create your clustered indexes.) But a non-clustered index includes only the key column values in the leaf nodes. For all other data, the optimizer must take additional steps to retrieve that data from elsewhere, which could represent significant overhead for your most common queries.

That's where the covering index comes in. When defining your non-clustered index, you can include columns in addition to the key columns.

For example, suppose one of your application's primary queries retrieves data from both the OrderID and OrderDate columns in the Sales table:

```
SELECT OrderID, OrderDate
FROM Sales
WHERE OrderID = 12345;
```

You can create a composite non-clustered index on both columns, but the OrderDate column only adds overhead to the index and serves no purpose as a key column. A better solution is to create a covering index with OrderID as the key column and OrderDate as the included column:

```
CREATE NON-CLUSTERED INDEX ix_orderid
ON dbo.Sales(OrderID)
INCLUDE (OrderDate);
```

This way, you avoid the disadvantages of indexing a column unnecessarily, while still benefiting your query. The included column is not part of the key, but the data is still stored in the leaf nodes. This can improve performance without incurring more overhead. Plus, there are fewer restrictions on columns used as included columns, compared to those used as key columns.

26. Does it matter how many duplicate values a key column contains?

Whenever you create an index, you should try to minimize the number of duplicate values contained in your key columns, or more precisely, try to keep the ratio of duplicate values as low as possible, when compared to the entire set of values.

If you're working with a composite index, that duplication refers to the key columns as a whole. The individual columns can contain lots of duplicates, but duplication across the columns should be at a minimum. For example, if you create a composite non-clustered index on the FirstName and LastName columns, you can have multiple John values and multiple Doe values, but you want to have as few John Doe values as possible, or better still, only one John Doe.

The ratio of unique values within a key column is referred to as index selectivity. The more unique the values, the higher the selectivity, which means that a unique index has the highest possible selectivity. The query engine loves highly selective key columns, especially if those columns are referenced in the WHERE clause of your frequently run queries. The higher the selectivity, the faster the query engine can reduce the size of the result set. The flipside, of course, is that a column with relatively few unique values is seldom a good candidate to be indexed.

27.Can you create a non-clustered index on a subset of data in your key column?

By default, a non-clustered index contains one row for every row in the table. Of course, you can say the same about a clustered index, given that the index is the table, but in terms of a non-clustered index, the one-to-one relationship is an important concept because, since SQL

Server 2008, you've been able to create filtered indexes that limit the rows included in the index.

A filtered index can improve query performance because it is smaller and includes filtered statistics, which are more accurate than full-table statistics, resulting in better execution plans. A filtered index also reduces storage and maintenance costs. The index is updated only when the applicable underlying data changes.

Be aware, however, that SQL Server places a number of restrictions on filtered indexes, such as not being able to create a filtered index on a view, so be sure to check out the SQL Server documentation.

CHAPTER 13 MVC QUESTIONS AND ANSWERS

1. What is MVC (Model View Controller)?

MVC is an architectural pattern which separates the representation from the interaction. It's divided into three broader sections: model, view, and controller. Below is how each one of them handles the task.

1. The view is responsible for the look and feel.

2. Model represents the real world object and provides data to the view.

3. The controller is responsible for taking the end user request and loading the appropriate model and view.

2. What is the difference between MVC and ASP.NET Web Forms?

ASP.NET Web Forms uses a page controller pattern approach for rendering layout, whereas MVC uses a front controller approach. In the case of the page controller approach, every page has its own controller, i.e., code-behind file that processes the request. On the other hand, in MVC, a common controller for all pages processes the requests.

3. What is the request flow in ASP.NET MVC framework?

A request hits the controller coming from client. The controller plays its role and decides which model to use in order to serve the request, further passing that model to a view, which then transforms the model and generates an appropriate response that is rendered to the client.

4. What is routing in MVC?

In case of a typical ASP.NET application, incoming requests are mapped to physical files such as .aspx file. The MVC framework uses friendly URLs that more easily describe a user's action but are not mapped to physical files.

The MVC framework uses a routing engine that maps URLs to controller classes. We can define routing rules for the engine, so that it can map incoming request URLs to an appropriate controller.

5. Can you explain the complete flow of MVC?

Below are the steps to control flows in MVC (Model, View, and controller) architecture:

• All end user requests are first sent to the controller.

• The controller depending on the request decides which model to load. The controller loads the model and attaches the model with the appropriate view.

• The final view is then attached with the model data and sent as a response to the client.

6. Is MVC suitable for both windows and web applications?

The MVC architecture is more suited to web applications than Windows Forms applications. For Window applications, MVP, i.e., "Model View Presenter" is more applicable. If you are using WPF and Silverlight, MVVM is more suitable due to the way bindings work.

7. What are the benefits of using MVC?

• Separation of concerns is achieved as we are moving the code-behind to a separate class file. By moving the binding code to a separate class file we promote reusability.

• Automated UI testing is possible because now the behind code (UI interaction code) has moved to a simple .NET class. This gives us opportunity to write unit tests and automate manual testing.

8. Is MVC different from a three layered architecture?

MVC is an evolution of a three layered traditional architecture. Many components of the three layered architecture are part of MVC.

9. What are html helpers in MVC?

HTML helpers are much like traditional ASP.NET Web Form controls. Just like web form controls in ASP.NET, HTML helpers are used to modify HTML, but HTML helpers are more lightweight. Unlike Web Form controls, an HTML helper does not have an event model or a view state. In most cases, an HTML helper is just a method that returns a string. With MVC, you can create your own helpers, or use the built in HTML helpers.

10. What is the difference between "HTML.TextBox" vs "HTML.TextBoxFor"?

Both of them provide the same HTML output. "HTML.TextBoxFor" is strongly typed while "HTML.TextBox" isn't.

11.What is the use of display modes?

View can be changed automatically based on display size, browser type, device type, etc.

12.Can we map multiple URL's to the same action?

Yes. You need to make two entries with different key names and specify the same controller and action.

13.How can we navigate from one view to another using a hyperlink?

By using the ActionLink method.

14.How can we restrict MVC actions to be invoked only to GET or POST?

Decorate the MVC action with the HttpGet or HttpPost attribute to restrict the type of HTTP calls allowed.

15.What are the difference between tempdata, viewdata, and viewbag?

Temp data - Helps to maintain data when you move from one controller to another or from one action to another. In other words, when you redirect, tempdata helps to maintain data between those redirects. It internally uses session variables.

View data - Helps to maintain data when you move from controller to view.

View Bag - It's a dynamic wrapper around view data. When you use Viewbag type, casting is not required. It uses the dynamic keyword internally.

16. What are partial views in MVC?

A partial view is a reusable view (like a user control) which can be embedded inside another view. Partial views have a .cshtml extension.

17. How do you create a partial view and consume it?

When you add a view to your project in Visual Studio you check the "Create partial view" check box. Once the partial view is created, call the partial view in the main view using the Html.RenderPartial() method.

18. How can we do validations in MVC?

One of the easiest ways of doing validation in MVC is by using data annotations. Data annotations are nothing but attributes which can be applied on model properties.

19. How to we display validation errors to the client?

In order to display the validation error message we need to use the ValidateMessageFor() method which belongs to the Html helper class.

20. How do you check to see if the model is valid in a particular controller method?

Call the ModelState.IsValid() or TryUpdateModel() methods.

21. Can we display all errors in one block?

Yes, we can; use the ValidationSummary() method from the Html helper class.

22. What are the other data annotation attributes for validation in MVC?

• StringLength.

• RegularExpression

• Range

• Compare

23. How do you add errors in the controller to a model?

Use the AddModelError() method.

24. How can we enable data annotation validation on the client side?

It's a two-step process: first reference the necessary jQuery files. Second, set the EnableClientValidation property to true in the web.config.

25. What is Razor in MVC?

It's a light weight view engine. Until MVC we had only one view type, i.e., ASPX. The Razor view engine was introduced in MVC 3.

26. Why Razor when we already have ASPX?

Razor is clean, lightweight, and its syntax is easy as compared to ASPX.

27. So which is a better fit, Razor or ASPX?

As per Microsoft, Razor is preferred because it is light weight and has a simpler syntax.

28. How can you do authentication and authorization in MVC?

You can use Windows or Forms authentication for MVC.

In the controller or on the action, you can use the Authorize attribute, which specifies which users have access to these controllers and actions. Now only the users specified in the controller and action can access it.

29.How do you implement Forms authentication in MVC?

Forms authentication is implemented the same way as in ASP.NET. The first step is to set the authentication mode equal to Forms. The loginUrl points to a controller here rather than a page.

We also need to create a controller where we will check if the user is authenticated or not. If the user is authenticated, we will set the cookie value.

30.What is the difference between ActionResult and ViewResult?

ActionResult is an abstract class while ViewResult derives from the ActionResult class. ActionResult has several derived classes like ViewResult, JsonResult, FileStreamResult, and so on.

ActionResult can be used to exploit polymorphism and dynamism. So if you are returning different types of views dynamically, ActionResult is best to use.

31. What are the different types of results in MVC?

There are 12 kinds of results in MVC. At the top is the ActionResult class which is a base class that can have 11 subtypes as listed below:

1. ViewResult - Renders a specified view to the response stream.

2. PartialViewResult - Renders a specified partial view to the response stream.

3. EmptyResult - An empty response is returned.

4. RedirectResult - Performs an HTTP redirection to a specified URL.

5. RedirectToRouteResult - Performs an HTTP redirection to a URL that is determined by the routing engine, based on given route data.

6. JsonResult - Serializes a given ViewData object to JSON format.

7. JavaScriptResult - Returns a piece of JavaScript code that can be executed on the client.

8. ContentResult - Writes content to the response stream without requiring a view.

9. FileContentResult - Returns a file to the client.

10. FileStreamResult - Returns a file to the client, which is provided by a Stream.

11. FilePathResult - Returns a file to the client.

32. What are ActionFilters in MVC?

ActionFilters help you to perform logic while an MVC action is executing or after an MVC action has executed. An action filter is an attribute. You can apply most action filters to either an individual controller action or an entire controller.

33. When are Action filters useful?

• Implement post-processing logic before the action happens.

• Cancel a current execution.

• Inspect the returned value.

• Provide extra data to the action.

34. What are some action filters in MVC?

• OutputCache – This action filter caches the output of a controller action for a specified amount of time.

• HandleError – This action filter handles errors raised when a controller action executes.

• Authorize – This action filter enables you to restrict access to a particular user or role.

35. How can you create action filters?

1. Create it Inline.

2. Create an ActionFilter attribute.

36. Can we create our custom view engine using MVC?

Yes, you can create your own custom view engine in MVC.

37. What is WebAPI?

WebAPI is the technology by which you can expose data over HTTP following REST principles.

38. What is bundling and minification in MVC?

Bundling and minification are two techniques to improve request load time. Bundling and minification improve load time by reducing the number of requests to the server and reducing the size of the requested assets through compression.

39. How does bundling increase performance?

Web projects always need CSS and script files. Bundling helps us combine multiple JavaScript and CSS files in to a single entity thus minimizing multiple requests into a single request.

40. So how do we implement bundling in MVC?

Open BundleConfig.cs from the App_Start folder.

41. How can you test bundling in debug mode?

If you are in a debug mode you need to set EnableOptimizations to true in the bundleconfig.cs file or else you will not see the bundling effect in the page requests.

42. Explain areas in MVC?

To accommodate large projects, ASP.NET MVC lets you partition web applications into smaller units that are referred to as areas. Areas provide a way to separate a large MVC web application into smaller functional groupings. An area is effectively an MVC structure inside an application. An application could contain several MVC structures (areas).

CHAPTER 14 ENTITY FRAMEWORK QUESTIONS AND ANSWERS

1. What is EF (Entity Framework)?

Entity Framework is an ORM (object relational mapping framework) which creates a higher abstract object model over ADO.NET components. So rather than getting into the DataSet, DataTable, Command and Connection objects, you work on higher level domain objects like customers, suppliers, etc.

2. What are the benefits of using EF (Entity Framework)?

The main benefit of EF is that it auto-generates code for the model (middle layer), data access layer, and maps code, thus reducing development time.

3. What are the different ways of creating these domain / entity objects?

Entity objects can be created in two ways: from a database structure or manually, called code first.

4. What is pluralize and singularize in the Entity Framework dialog box?

"Pluralize" and "Singularize" give meaningful naming conventions to objects. In simple words, it asks which naming convention you want to use when naming objects:

• One Customer record means "Customer" (singular).

• Lot of customer records means "Customer's" (plural, watch the "s")

5. What is the importance of EDMX file in Entity Framework?

EDMX (Entity Data Model XML) is an XML file which contains all the mapping details of how your objects map with SQL tables. The EDMX file is further divided into three sections: CSDL, SSDL, and MSL.

6. Can you explain CSDL, SSDL and MSL sections in an EDMX file?

• CSDL (Conceptual Schema definition language) is the conceptual abstraction which is exposed to the application.

• SSDL (Storage Schema Definition Language) defines the mapping with your RDBMS data structure.

• MSL (Mapping Schema Language) connects the CSDL and SSDL. CSDL, SSDL and MSL are actually XML files.

7. What are T4 templates?

T4 (Text Template Transformation Toolkit) is a template based code generation engine. You can go and write C# code in T4 templates (.tt is the extension) files and those C# codes execute to generate the file as per the written C# logic.

8. What is the importance of T4 in the Entity Framework?

T4 files are the heart of EF code generation. The T4 code templates read the EDMX XML file and generate C# behind code. This C# behind code is nothing but your entity and context classes.

9. How can we read records using Entity Framework classes?

In order to browse through records, you create the object of the context class and inside the context class you will get the records.

10.How can we add, update, and delete using EF?

Create the object of your entity class, add it to the data context using AddObject method, and then call the SaveChanges method. If you want to update, select the object, make changes to the object and call AcceptAllChanges. If you want to delete, call the DeleteObject method.

11.Why would anyone say the Entity Framework runs slow?

By default, EF has lazy loading behavior. Due to this default behavior if you are loading a large number of records and especially if they have foreign key relationships, you can have performance issues. So you need to be cautious and understand if you really need lazy loading behavior for all scenarios. For better performance, disable lazy loading when you are loading a large number of records or use stored procedures.

12.What does lazy loading refer to?

Lazy loading is a concept where we load objects on demand rather than loading everything upfront. Entity Framework has lazy loading behavior enabled by default.

13.How can we turn off lazy loading?

The opposite of lazy loading is eager loading. In eager loading we load the objects beforehand. To disable lazy loading set LazyLoadingEnabled to false.

14.What are POCO classes in Entity Framework?

POCO means Plain Old C# Object. When EDMX creates classes, they are cluttered with a lot of entity tags. You can create a simple .NET class and use the entity context object to load your simple .NET classes.

15.How do we implement POCO in Entity Framework?

To implement POCO is a three step process:

1. Go to the designer and set the code generation strategy to NONE. This step means that you would be generating the classes on your own rather than relying on EF auto code generation.

2. Now that auto generation of code is disabled, create the domain classes manually. Add a class file and create the domain classes.

3. Finally, use the created code in your client as if you were using EF normally.

16. In POCO classes do we need EDMX files?

Yes, you will still need EDMX files because the context object reads the EDMX files to do the mapping.

17. What is the code first approach in Entity Framework?

In code first approach we avoid working with the Visual Designer of Entity Framework. In other words, the EDMX file is excluded from the solution. So you now have complete control over the context class as well as the entity classes.

18. What is the difference between POCO, Code First, and simple EF approach?

All these three approaches define how much control you want on your Entity Framework code.

Entity Framework is an object relational mapper. It generates a middle tier (Entity) and a data access layer (Context).

In simple Entity Framework, everything is auto generated and so you need the EDMX XML file as well. POCO is semi-automatic so you have full control on the entity classes but then the context classes are still generated by the EDMX file.

In Code First, you have complete control on how you can create the entity and context classes. Because you are going to manually create these classes, you do not have dependency on the EDMX XML file.

19. What is optimistic locking and pessimistic locking?

Optimistic Locking

Optimistic Locking is a strategy where you read a record, take note of a version number, timestamp or state of a row and check that change has not happened before you write the record back. When you write the record back you filter the update on the version to make sure it's atomic. (i.e. hasn't been updated between when you check the version and write the record to the disk) and update the version in one hit.

If the record is dirty (i.e. different version than yours) you abort the transaction and the user can re-start it.

This strategy is most applicable to high-volume systems and three-tier architectures where you do not necessarily maintain a connection to the database for your session. In this situation the client cannot actually maintain database locks as the connections are taken from a pool and you may not be using the same connection from one access to the next.

Pessimistic locking

Pessimistic locking is when you lock a record for exclusive use until you have finished with it. It promotes better integrity than optimistic locking but requires one to be careful with your application design to avoid deadlocks. To use pessimistic locking you need either a direct connection to the database (as would typically be the case in a two tier client server application) or an externally available transaction ID that can be used independently of the connection.

In the latter case you open the transaction with the TxID and then reconnect using that ID. The DBMS maintains the locks and allows you to pick the session back up through the TxID. This is how distributed transactions using two-phase commit protocols (such as XA or COM+ Transactions) work.

20. How can we handle concurrency in the Entity Framework?

In EF, concurrency issues are resolved by using optimistic locking. To implement optimistic locking, right click on the EDMX designer and set the concurrency mode to "Fixed".

21. How can we use pessimistic locking in the Entity Framework?

We can't use pessimistic locking when using the Entity Framework. You can invoke a stored procedure from within the Entity Framework and do pessimistic locking by setting the isolation level in the stored procedure. But directly, Entity Framework does not support pessimistic locking.

22. What is client wins and store wins mode in Entity Framework concurrency?

Client wins and store wins are actions taken during concurrent access. In store wins/database wins, the data from the server is loaded into your entity objects. Client wins is opposite to store wins. Data from your entity object is saved to the database.

23. What are scalar and navigation properties in Entity Framework?

Scalar properties have actual values contained in the entities. Normally a scalar property will map to a database field.

Navigation properties help to navigate from one entity to another entity. Navigation properties are automatically created from the primary and foreign key references.

24. What are complex types in Entity Framework?

Types containing common properties used across multiple entities. To create a complex type, select the fields which you want to group in a complex type, click on "Refactor", and create the complex type.

25. What's the difference between LINQ to SQL and Entity Framework?

• LINQ to SQL is good for rapid development with SQL Server. EF is for enterprise scenarios and works with SQL Server as well as other databases.

• LINQ maps directly to tables. One LINQ entity class maps to one table. EF has a conceptual model and that conceptual model maps to the storage model via mappings. So one EF class can map to multiple tables or one table can map to multiple classes.

• LINQ is more targeted towards developing a loosely coupled framework.

26. What is the difference between DbContext and ObjectContext?

DbContext is a wrapper around ObjectContext. It is a simplified version of ObjectContext. As a developer you can start with DbContext as it is simpler to use. When you feel that some of the operations cannot be achieved by DbContext, you can then access ObjectContext from DbContext.

CHAPTER 15 WCF AND WEB SERVICES QUESTIONS AND ANSWERS

1. What is SOA?

Service-oriented architecture (SOA) is a software design and software architecture design pattern based on discrete pieces of software providing application functionality as services to other applications. This is known as service-orientation. It is independent of any vendor, product or technology.

2. What is the difference between a service and a component?

A service can be made up of several components. Usually a service provides one complete feature that is made up by combining different components. The client doesn't need to know anything about the underlying components. The client will deal directly with the service while the service will be interacting with the components internally.

3. What are basic steps to create a WCF service?

1. Create a service contract.

2. Expose endpoints with metadata.

3. Implement the service definition.

4. Consume the service.

4. What are endpoints, addresses, contracts and bindings in WCF?

All communication with a Windows Communication Foundation (WCF) service occurs through the endpoints of the service. Endpoints provide clients access to the functionality offered by a WCF service.

Each endpoint consists of four properties:

1. An address that indicates where the endpoint can be found.

2. A binding that specifies how a client can communicate with the endpoint.

3. A contract that identifies the operations available.

4. A set of behaviors that specify local implementation details of the endpoint.

5. What are various ways of hosting a WCF service?

There are four common ways:

1. Hosting in IIS

2. Hosting in WAS (Windows Application Service in IIS 7+)

3. Hosting in a Windows service

4. Hosting in an application (aka "self-hosting"). E.g. A console application.

6. What are some benefits of hosting a WCF service in IIS?

• Built-in logging, application pool scaling, throttling and configuration of your site

• Built-in features allow for population of context classes with information and state. i.e. HttpContext

• Built-in security features. i.e. Authorization

• Memory recycling features when processes fail or based on time interval.

7. What is the difference between BasicHttpBinding and WsHttpBinding?

One of the biggest differences is the security aspect. By default, BasicHttpBinding sends data in plain text while WsHttpBinding sends it in an encrypted and secured manner.

8. How can we do debugging and tracing in WCF?

You can debug the WCF service as you do any other web application. Configuring tracing is enabled from the web.config.

9. What is a transaction in WCF?

A transaction is a logical unit of work consisting of multiple activities that need to all succeed or all fail, otherwise any work that was done is rolled back. Transaction attributes can be applied to methods within a service contract and implemented within the service definition.

10.How can we self-host a WCF service?

To host a service inside a managed application, embed the code for the service inside the managed application code, define an endpoint for the service either imperatively in code, declaratively through configuration, or using default endpoints, and then create an instance of ServiceHost.

11. What are some different ways of implementing WCF Security?

1) Transport level security

2) Message security, or

3) Identity and role based security.

12. How can one implement SSL security in WCF?

Utilizing transport level security via a web.config configuration or proper setup in an IIS hosted service.

13. What are the system provided bindings in WCF?

- BasicHttpBinding

- WSHttpBinding

- WSDualHttpBinding

- WSFederationHttpBinding

- NetHttpBinding

- NetHttpsBinding

- NetTcpBinding

- NetNamedPipeBinding

- NetMsmqBinding

- NetPeerTcpBinding

- MsmqIntegrationBinding

- BasicHttpContextBinding

- NetTcpContextBinding

- WebHttpBinding

- WSHttpContextBinding

- UdpBinding

14.What are the different WCF instancing modes?

Per Call, Per Session and Single instance mode.

15.Explain the "Per Call" instance mode?

When we configure a WCF service as per call, new service instances are created for every method call you make via a WCF proxy client.

16. Where does one specify the instancing mode for a WCF service?

In order to specify the instancing mode, we need to provide the InstanceContextMode value in the ServiceBehavior attribute on the Service definition class.

17. What are the 3 WCF InstanceContextModes and when would you each?

1) Per call

• You want a stateless services

• Your service hold intensive resources like connection object and huge memory objects.

• Scalability is a prime requirement. You would like to have scale out architecture.

• Your WCF functions are called in a single threaded model.

2) Per session

• You want to maintain states between WCF calls.

• You want ok with a Scale up architecture.

• Light resource references

3) Single

• You want share global data through your WCF service.

• Scalability is not a concern.

18.What are the 3 WCF concurrency types?

1. Single: A single request has access to the WCF service object at a given moment of time. So only one request will be processed at any given moment of time. The other requests have to wait until the request processed by the WCF service is completed.

2. Multiple: In this scenario, multiple requests can be handled by the WCF service object at any given moment of time. In other words, requests are processed at the same time by spawning multiple threads on the WCF server object. So you have great throughput here but you need to ensure concurrency issues related to WCF server objects.

4. Reentrant: A single request thread has access to the WCF service object, but the thread can exit the WCF service to call another WCF service or can also call a WCF client through callback and reenter without deadlock.

19.What is throttling behavior in a WCF service?

WCF throttling helps you to put an upper limit on the number of concurrent calls, WCF instances, and concurrent sessions. WCF provides three ways by which you can define upper limits: MaxConcurrentCalls, MaxConcurrentInstances, and MaxConcurrentSessions.

20. What is SOAP?

SOAP stands for "Simple Object Access Protocol". SOAP is a lightweight protocol intended for exchanging structured information in a decentralized, distributed environment. SOAP uses XML technologies to define an extensible messaging framework, which provides a message construct that can be exchanged over a variety of underlying protocols. The framework has been designed to be independent of any particular programming model and other implementation specific semantics.

21. What is the difference between SOAP and REST services?

SOAP and REST can't be compared directly, since the first is a protocol (or at least tries to be) and the second is an architectural style. This is probably one of the biggest sources of confusion around comparing the two. People tend to call REST any HTTP API that isn't SOAP.

The main difference between SOAP and REST is the degree of coupling between client and server implementations. A SOAP client works like a custom desktop application, tightly coupled to the server. There's a rigid contract between client and server, and everything is expected to break if either side changes anything. You need constant updates following any change.

Important points to understand what REST is about, and how it differs from SOAP:

• REST is protocol independent. It's not coupled to HTTP. A REST application can use any protocol for which there is a standardized URI scheme.

• REST is not mapping CRUD to HTTP methods.

• REST is as standardized as the parts you're using. Security and authentication in HTTP is standardized, so that's what you use when doing REST over HTTP.

• REST is not REST without HATEOAS (Hypermedia as the Engine of Application State). This means that a client only knows the entry point URI and the resources are supposed to return links the client should follow.

22. What is HATEOAS?

HATEOAS is an abbreviation for "Hypermedia as the Engine of Application State". It is a constraint of the REST application architecture that distinguishes it from most other network application architectures. The principle is that a client interacts with a network application entirely through hypermedia provided dynamically by application servers. A REST client needs no prior knowledge about how to interact with any particular application or server beyond a generic understanding of hypermedia. By contrast, in a service-oriented architecture (SOA), clients and servers interact through a fixed interface shared through documentation or an interface description language (IDL). The HATEOAS constraint decouples client and server in a way that allows the server functionality to evolve independently.

23. What is WSDL?

It means Web Services Description Language. It is the service description layer in the web service protocol stock. The Service Description layer describes the user interface to a web service.

24. What UDDI means?

UDDI stands for Universal, Description, Discovery, and Integration. It is the discovery layer in the web services protocol stack.

25. What is REST?

REST stands for Representational State Transfer. (It is sometimes spelled "ReST".) It relies on a stateless, client-server, cacheable communications protocol -- and in virtually all cases, the HTTP protocol is used. REST is an architecture style for designing networked applications.

26. What are the six constraints of the REST architectural style?

1) Uniform Interface

2) Stateless

3) Cacheable

4) Client-Server

5) Layered System

6) Code on Demand

27. What Is DISCO?

DISCO means discovery. It groups interrelated web services. The organization that provides web services, issues a DISCO file on its server and that file contains the links of all the provided web services. This standard is good when the client knows the company already. It can be used within a local network as well.

28. What are some differences between .NET Web Services and .NET Remoting?

• The key difference between ASP.NET Web Services and .NET Remoting is in how they serialize data into messages and the format they choose for metadata.

• ASP.NET Web services favor the XML Schema type system, and provide a simple programming model with broad cross-platform reach. .NET Remoting favors the runtime type system, and provides a more complex programming model having a more limited reach.

29. What are some aspects of ASP.NET state management?

The ASP.NET Web Services model assumes stateless service architecture by default; it does not inherently correlate multiple calls from the same user. In addition, each time a client invokes an ASP.NET Web Service, a new object is created to service the request.

CHAPTER 16 SILVERLIGHT QUESTIONS AND ANSWERS

1. What is Microsoft Silverlight?

• Silverlight is a web based technology, launched by Microsoft in April 2007. Silverlight is considered as a competitor to Adobe's Flash.

• Silverlight is Microsoft's implementation of a cross-browser, cross-platform client framework that allows designers and developers to deliver Rich Internet Applications (RIA) embedded in Web pages.

• Silverlight is a browser plug-in approximately 6MB in size; it is client-side free software, with an easy and fast (less than 10 sec) one-time installation available for any client side browser.

• It supports advanced data integration, multithreading, HD video using IIS Smooth Streaming, and built-in content protection. Silverlight enables online and offline applications for a broad range of business and consumer scenarios.

• One of the design goals of the Silverlight technology is to fill the gap between Windows applications and Web applications in terms of creating Graphical User Interfaces (GUI).

• Silverlight applications are run as client-side applications without the need to refresh the browser to update the UI. However, because of the built-in .NET framework, Silverlight applications can easily integrate with server-side controls and services. Using Silverlight's implementation of the .NET framework, developers can easily integrate existing libraries and code into Silverlight applications.

2. Why architect an application in Silverlight?

• Support for the .NET Framework – if you are already a .NET developer, it is easy to start programming in Silverlight.

• Support for managed code – you can write programs in your favorite language which .NET CLR supports like C#, VB.NET, dynamic languages (IronPython, IronRuby).

• Better development tools -Visual Studio 2010, Expression Blend.

• Large community- More learning resources available compared to Flash.

• Integration with Enterprise based technologies like WPF, LINQ etc.

• Silverlight integrates the XAML declarative language with the .NET framework.

• It is a cross-browser, cross-platform technology which provides a consistent user experience everywhere it runs.

• The Silverlight plug-in installs in seconds, and leaves a very small footprint.

• After you install the plug-in, users no longer need to install anything on their workstations to run Silverlight applications. The applications are available to them from whatever browser they are accessing.

• It runs a client-side application that can read data and update the UI without interrupting the user by refreshing the whole page.

• It can run asynchronous communications with the server, allowing the UI to continue to function while waiting for the server response.

• It delivers rich video, audio, and graphics.

3. Is Silverlight free?

Yes, Microsoft has made the Silverlight browser plug-in freely available for all supported platforms and browsers.

4. What is Silverlight Runtime?

Silverlight Runtime is a browser plug-in to support Silverlight enabled applications.

5. What is a .xap file?

A .xap file is a Silverlight-based application package (.xap) that is generated when the Silverlight project is built. A .xap file is the compressed output file for a Silverlight application. The .xap file includes AppManifest.xaml, the compiled output assembly of the Silverlight project (.dll), and the resource files referred to by the Silverlight application.

6. What is a Silverlight.js file?

Silverlight.js is a helper file which enables websites to create advanced Silverlight installation and instantiation experiences. You can call the createObject and createObjectEx functions defined in this file to embed the Silverlight plug-in in a web page.

7. What is the use of the ClientBin folder?

The ClientBin folder is used to place the .xap file of a Silverlight application. You can keep it anywhere in your web application, but this is the default location used by Silverlight.

8. How would you change the default page of a Silverlight application?

To change the default page of a Silverlight application, you need to set the RootVisual property inside the Application_Startup event of the App.xaml file.

9. What is XAML?

XAML stands for eXtended Application Markup Language. XAML contains XML that is used to declaratively specify the user interface for Silverlight or WPF applications.

10. What is the AppManifest.xml file?

The AppManifest.xml file defines the assemblies that get deployed in the client application. This file is automatically updated when compiling your application (including the Runtime version information). Based on the settings of a referenced assembly it is added to the Application manifest.

11.What files are contained within the .xap file?

The .xap file contains an application manifest (AppManifest.xaml) file and all the necessary DLLs that are required by the application.

12.Can I consume WCF and ASP.NET Web Services in Silverlight?

Yes

13.What is the difference between WPF and Silverlight?

Silverlight and Windows Presentation Foundation (WPF) are two different products from Microsoft, but have lot of overlap. Silverlight is a subset of WPF in terms of features and functionality.

Silverlight is a Microsoft technology, competing with Adobe's Flash, and is meant for developing rich browser based internet applications.

WPF is a Microsoft technology meant for developing enhanced graphics applications for the desktop platform. In addition, WPF applications can be hosted on web browsers which offer rich graphics features for web applications. Web Browser Applications (WBA) developed on the WPF technology uses XAML to host user interfaces for browser applications. XAML stands for eXtended Application Markup Language, which is a new declarative programming model from Microsoft. XAML files are hosted as discrete files in the Web server, but are downloaded to the browsers and converted to a user interface by the .NET runtime in the client browsers.

WPF runs on the .NET runtime, and developers can take advantage of the rich .NET Framework and WPF libraries to build really cool Windows applications. WPF supports 3-D graphics, complex animations, hardware acceleration etc.

Silverlight uses a particular implementation of a XAML parser, with that parser being part of the Silverlight core installation. In some cases, the parsing behavior differs from the parsing behavior in Windows Presentation Foundation (WPF), which also has a particular implementation.

14. *What are the different layout controls available in Silverlight?*

There are three different types of layout controls provided by Silverlight:

1. Canvas - Position child elements absolutely in x, y space.

2. StackPanel - Position child elements relative to one another in horizontal or vertical stacks.

3. Grid - Position child elements in rows and columns.

15.Do I need to have the .NET Framework installed in order to use Silverlight?

The answer to this is no - a cross platform version of the .NET Framework is included in the 6 MB Silverlight 4 download, which means you do not need to have anything extra installed on the client in order to access Silverlight applications in the browser.

16.What is meant by RIA?

RIA stands for Rich Internet Applications, which are Web applications with rich user interfaces including media elements such as audio, video etc. You can think of them as being similar to powerful and rich desktop applications, except that RIA applications are Web based.

17.What are the design files and the code-behind files in Silverlight?

The user interface elements of Silverlight applications are defined in XAML files. The logic and functionality of

Silverlight applications is implemented using managed .NET code-behind files that share the same class with the XAML file.

18. What are .NET RIA Services?

Microsoft .NET RIA Services help to simplify the n-tier application pattern by combining the ASP.NET and Silverlight platforms. RIA Services provides a "pattern" which allows one to write application logic that can run on the mid-tier and controls access to data for queries, changes, and custom operations. It also provides support for data validation, authentication, and roles by integrating with Silverlight components on the client and ASP.NET on the middle tier.

RIA services is a server-side technology that automatically generates client-side (Silverlight) objects that take care of the communication with the server for you and provide client-side validation.

CHAPTER 17 WPF QUESTIONS AND ANSWERS

1. What is WPF?

Microsoft introduced the WPF (Windows Presentation Foundation) API as part of the .NET 3.0 framework. WPF merged all of the unrelated APIs into a single unified object model. So if you want to use 3D graphics or multimedia for your application, you don't need to use different APIs. WPF provides all the functionalities you need to develop richer GUI applications. Using WPF we can develop GUI's for both windows applications and web applications.

2. What are some advantages of WPF over Windows forms applications?

• Supports 2D and 3D vector graphics.

• Animation

• Multimedia

- Fixed and Flow format documents

- Having all capabilities of Html and Flash.

- The UI is separated from logic code.

3. What is XAML?

XAML (pronounced Zammel) is a declarative XML-based language by which you can define objects and properties in XML.

4. What are attached properties?

These are dependency properties that belong to one class but can be used in another.

5. What class does every visually represented element derive from?

Each and every element that has visual representation and appears in a WPF Window is derived from the **Visual** class.

6. What threading model does WPF use?

Single-threaded

7. What is the use of the "System.Windows.Markup" namespace in WPF?

The System.Windows.Markup namespace provides helper classes for XAML code.

8. Which namespace provides classes for integration with WPF and Win32?

The "System.Windows.Interop" namespace provides classes for integration of WPF with Win32.

9. Which class is the base class of all the visual elements of WPF?

Control

10. The Control class of WPF is derived from which class?

FrameworkElement

11. What is the 'One-way-to-Source ' binding property?

When the target property changes, the source object gets updated.

12. Which namespace is used to work with 3D in WPF?

System.Windows.Media.Media3D

13. What are XBAP's?

Xml Browser Applications (XBAP) are WPF applications which run with an .xbap extension in the browser.

14. Is it possible for a control to define a handler for an event that the control cannot itself raise?

Yes, via attached events.

15. What is the difference between User Settings and Application Settings in WPF?

User Settings are can be read or write even at runtime and can be saved. The Application Settings are read-only; they can only be written to at design time.

16. What is a routed event?

A typical WPF application contains many elements. These elements exist in an element tree relationship with each other. A routed event is a type of event that can invoke handlers on multiple listeners in an element tree, rather than just on the object that raised the event.

17. What is style Inheritance?

It is the technique through which one style acquires the features of another style. It is implemented through the BasedOn property of the Style class.

18. What is x:Code?

x:Code is a directive element defined in XAML. An x:Code directive element can contain inline programming code. The code that is defined inline can interact with the XAML on the same page.

19. What are the core WPF assemblies?

WindowsBase.dll:- It defines the core types constituting the infrastructure of WPF API.

PresentationCore.dll:- Defines numerous types constituting foundation of WPF GUI layer.

PresentationFoundation.dll:- It defines WPF control types, animation & multimedia support, data binding support and other WPF services.

Besides these three libraries WPF also uses an unmanaged binary called milcore.dll which acts as a bridge between WPF assemblies and DirectX runtime layer.

20.What is the use of System.Windows.Media namespace?

It is the root namespace to several other media related namespaces. It provides different types to work with animations, 3D rendering, text rendering and other multimedia services.

21.How does one implement threading in WPF?

The most common way is to use BackgroundWorker or Async.

22.What are the two responsibilities of the DispatcherObject class?

The DispatcherObject class has two chief duties: to provide access to the current Dispatcher that an object is tied to and provide methods to check (CheckAccess) and verify (VerifyAccess) that a thread has access to an object (derived from DispatcherObject).

23.Explain UpdateSourceTrigger in WPF?

UpdateSourceTrigger is a property of a binding element in WPF. This Property defines the timing of binding source updates. There are two binding modes which updates the source, OneWayToSource and TwoWay.

24. What are the three values the UpdateSourceTrigger property can have?

1. LostFocus

2. PropertyChanged

3. Explicit

25. Explain the three graphics rendering modes i.e. Tier 0, Tier 1 and Tier 2?

• Rendering Tier 0: No graphics hardware acceleration. All graphics features use software acceleration. The DirectX version level is less than version 9.0.

• Rendering Tier 1: Some graphics features use graphics hardware acceleration. The DirectX version level is greater than or equal to version 9.0.

• Rendering Tier 2: Most graphics features use graphics hardware acceleration. The DirectX version level is greater than or equal to version 9.0.

26. What are the 3 layers that define the architecture of WPF?

The Common Language Runtime (CLR) is the base followed by the PresentationCore layer followed by the PresentationFramework layer.

27. What are the types of templates available in WPF?

• Data Templates: Data Template visual representation of data in control with style-like list box.

• Control Templates: Control Template suppliers a visual representation of a UI Control like Button or List View.

• Items Panel Templates: Item Panel Templates uses when we want to show data in Hierarchical way like child object use under parent object.

28. What are the different data binding modes in WPF?

• OneWay: The target is updated when the source changes.

• TwoWay: The target is updated when the source changes, and similarly, the source is updated when the target changes.

• OneWayToSource: Only the source is updated when the target changes.

• OneTime: The target is updated only the first time the source changes.

29. What is the importance of INotifyPropertyChanged in WPF?

This interface contains a single event called "PropertyChanged" of the delegate type "PropertyChangedEventHandler". It notifies the WPF/Silverlight framework whenever the value of a property changes in an object and fires the event in the "set" accessor of the property.

30. What is the importance of INotifyCollectionChanged in WPF?

This interface is similar to INotifyPropertyChanged. It notifies the WPF/Silverlight framework whenever any changes occur in a collection, like adding an object or deleting an object.

An "ObservableCollection" is a built-in class which implements the INotifyCollectionChanged interface.

31. What is the logical tree in WPF?

The logical tree describes the relationship between elements of the user interface. Every aspect of WPF (properties, events, resources, and so on) has behavior tied to the logical tree.

The logical tree is responsible for:

• Inheriting dependency property values.

• Resolving dynamic resource references.

• Looking up element names for bindings.

• Forwarding routed events.

32. What is the visual tree in WPF?

The visual tree is an expansion of the logical tree in which nodes are broken down into their visual components.

The visual tree contains all logical elements including all visual elements. The elements that appear in a visual tree derive from"'System.Windows.Media.Visual" and "System.Windows.Media.Visual3D".

The visual tree is responsible for:

1. Rendering visual elements.

2. Propagating element opacity.

3. Propagating layout and rendering transforms.

4. Propagating the 'IsEnabled' property.

33. What are dependency properties and their use in WPF?

• Dependency properties are used to enable styling, automatic data binding, templates, animation etc.

• All types that want to use DependencyProperties must derive from "DependencyObject" class.

• The value of a DependencyProperty is resolved dynamically when read.

• The value of a dependency property is stored in a dictionary of keys and values provided by "DependencyObject" class.

34. What are some advantages of dependency properties?

1. Reduced memory footprint

2. Value inheritance

3. Change notification

35. What types of resources are utilized in WPF?

1. Binary Resources

2. Logical Resources (Static and Dynamic Resources)

36. What are static resources?

A resource is an object that can be reused in different places in your application. Examples of resources include brushes and styles. StaticResources are resolved at compile time. Use StaticResources when it is clear that you do not need your resource re-evaluated during the lifetime of the application. A static resource performs better than dynamic resources.

37. What are dynamics resources?

DynamicResources are resolved at runtime. Use DynamicResources when the value of the resource could change during the lifetime of the application.

38. What are triggers?

Triggers are objects that enable you to apply changes when certain conditions (such as when a certain property value becomes true, or when an event occurs) are satisfied. Triggers define a list of setters that are executed if the specified condition is fulfilled.

39. What are some types of triggers?

• Property triggers get active when a property gets a specified value.

• Data triggers get active when a specified event is fired.

• Event triggers get active when a binding expression reaches a specified value.

40. What is the application object and its responsibility?

Application is a class that represents a WPF application running as a standalone client application in Windows. Each running application contains of at most a single instance of Application. The Application object is defined in the App.xaml file and is responsible for:

• Managing application lifetime (e.g. responding to startup/shutdown events)

• Window, property and resource management

• Command-line processing

• Navigation

41. What is the Application Lifetime in WPF?

• Startup – Application is starting up.

• Exit – Fired when an application is shutting down.

• Activated – Fired when an application gets focus, i.e. becomes the foreground application.

• Deactivated – Fired when application loses focus, i.e. is no longer the foreground application.

• DispatcherUnhandledException – Fired when an exception is thrown, but not yet handled. You can choose to handle the exception or not.

• SessionEnding – Fired when Windows is being shut down–due to either logoff or Windows shutdown. You can cancel the shutdown sequence.

42. What is the series of window events at startup in a WPF application?

At application startup, the Window events that are fired (in order) for the main window are:

1. Initialized - Main window is being created.

2. IsVisibleChanged - IsVisible property set to true.

4. SizeChanged - Size property set to size of window.

5. LayoutUpdated - Window layout changes.

6. SourceInitialized - Window is attached to Win32 window handle.

7. Activated - Window becomes foreground window.

8. PreviewGotKeyboardFocus - Window getting focus.

9. IsKeyboardFocusWithinChanged - IsKeyboardFocusWithin property set to true.

10. IsKeyboardFocusedChanged - IsKeyboardFocused property set to true.

11. GotKeyboardFocus - Window now has keyboard focus.

12. LayoutUpdated - Window layout changes.

13. Loaded - Window is now laid out, fully rendered.

14. ContentRendered - All window content has been rendered.

43. What is the series of event fired for application shutdown in WPF?

1. Closing - Window is going to close

2. IsVisibleChanged - IsVisible property set to false

3. Deactivated - Window becomes background window

4. IsKeyboardFocusWithinChanged - IsKeyboardFocusWithin property set to false

5. IsKeyboardFocusedChanged - IsKeyboardFocused property set to false

6. LostKeyboardFocus - Window no longer has keyboard focus

7. Closed - Window is closing

44.What's an EventAggregator?

A service that is primarily a container for events that allows publishers and subscribers to be decoupled so they can evolve independently. This decoupling is useful in modularized applications because new modules can be added that respond to events defined by the shell or other modules.

CHAPTER 18 SECURITY QUESTIONS AND ANSWERS

1. ***What is the difference between Symmetric and Asymmetric encryption?***

Symmetric Encryption (Also called secret key encryption)

Symmetric encryption is the oldest and best-known technique of encrypting data. A secret key, which can be a number, a word, or just a string of random letters, is applied to the text of a message to change the content in a particular way. This might be as simple as shifting each letter by a number of places in the alphabet. As long as both sender and recipient know the secret key, they can encrypt and decrypt all messages that use this key.

The problem with secret keys is exchanging them over the Internet or a large network, while preventing them from falling into the wrong hands. Anyone who knows the secret key can decrypt the message.

Asymmetric Encryption **(Also called public key encryption)**

Asymmetric encryption, in which there are two related keys--a key pair. A public key is made freely available to anyone who might want to send you a message. A second, private key is kept secret, so that only you know it.

Any message (text, binary files, or documents) that are encrypted by using the public key can only be decrypted by applying the same algorithm, but by using the matching private key. Any message that is encrypted by using the private key can only be decrypted by using the matching public key.

This means that you don't have to worry about passing public keys over the Internet (the keys are supposed to be public). A problem with asymmetric encryption, however, is that it is slower than symmetric encryption. It requires far more processing power to both encrypt and decrypt the content of the message.

2. *What is a fundamental difference between a hash algorithm and an encryption algorithm?*

A hash algorithm provides a one-way encryption of data. You cannot convert data back to its original form.

Encryption is two-way – The data can be decrypted if you have the correct decryption key.

Ending Notes

At this point you should be a programming god or at least a C# technical interviewing master.

Remember, don't just memorize the answer without a thorough understanding of the concepts that lie behind it. The best programmers aren't always the smartest ones. The best programmers are the ones who spend the countless hours and days understanding, not only the language, but the concepts that the language conveys. The language allows the programmer to implement abstractions. It's those abstractions that must be fully understood in order to implement the best applications.

If you're asked a great interview question and want to share it, feel free to contact me at the address in the beginning of this book.

Lastly, if this book helped you out, help me out and give this book an awesome review on Amazon.com or any other book selling website. Tell a co-worker or friend and spread the word. I write these books to help prepare you to get the most money possible.

Thanks for reading, I appreciate it.

Made in the USA
Lexington, KY
09 February 2017